Hoosier Hospitality

Favorite Recipes From Indiana's Finest Bed & Breakfast Inns

Tracy & Phyllis Winters

Winters Publishing
P.O. Box 501
Greensburg, Indiana   47240

800-457-3230
812-663-4948

Cover photo by: E. Anthony Valainis
Courtesy of: Frederick-Talbott Inn

The information about the inns and the recipes were supplied by the inns themselves. The rate information was current at the time of submission, but is subject to change. Every effort has been made to assure that the book is accurate. Neither the editors, The Indiana Bed & Breakfast Association, the individual inns or the publisher assume responsibility for any errors, whether typographical or otherwise.

Library of Congress Card Catalog Number 97-90380
ISBN 1-883651-07-7

Preface

We trust that you will enjoy sampling some of the recipes in this copy of *Hoosier Hospitality*. We also invite you to take a journey to some of the fine Indiana inns which are included.

We have endeavored to provide you with an error-free cookbook, and although the recipes included have been tested at each of the Bed and Breakfasts, they were not specifically tested for this cookbook. These recipes represent some of the personal favorites of the innkeepers, and we are proud to bring them to you.

We hope that you enjoy *Hoosier Hospitality*. Please visit some of the inns featured inside and enjoy warm hospitality and delicious food.

Rates

We have used the following symbols to represent the price range of the Bed & Breakfast Inns:

$ - $50 or less
$$ - $51 to $75
$$$ - $76 to $100
$$$$ - more than $100

Please call ahead to verify rates and room availability.

CONTENTS

1877 House Country Inn 6

Ahlbrand's Inn 10

Arbor Hill Inn 12

Atwater Century Farm Bed & Breakfast 14

Bauer House Bed & Breakfast 16

Bee Hive Bed & Breakfast 18

The Beiger Mansion Inn 20

The Big House in the Little Woods Bed & Breakfast 22

The Book Inn Bed & Breakfast 24

The Carole Lombard House 26

Cole House Bed & Breakfast 28

The Country Victorian Bed & Breakfast 30

Dunes Shore Inn Bed & Breakfast 32

Empty Nest Bed & Breakfast 34

The Folke Family Farm Inn 36

The Frederick-Talbott Inn 38

Gray Goose Inn 40

Hill Top Country Inn 44

The Hutchinson Mansion Inn 46

Indian Creek Bed & Breakfast 48

The Inn at Aberdeen 50

Inn at Bethlehem 52

Kati-Scarlett Bed & Breakfast 56

Lanning House & 1920's Annex 58

The Lookout Country Inn 60

M & N Bed & Breakfast 62

Market Street Guest House 64

McCray Mansion Inn Bed & Breakfast 66

Mulberry Inn & Gardens Bed & Breakfast 68

The Nuthatch Bed & Breakfast 70

Oak Haven Bed & Breakfast 72

Oakwood Bed & Breakfast......................................74

The Old Northside Bed & Breakfast 76

Olde Buffalo Inn Bed & Breakfast......................................78

The Oliver Inn Bed & Breakfast 80

Orchard Hill Inn & Cabin......................................84

The Prairie House Bed & Breakfast 86

Prairie Manor Bed & Breakfast......................................88

Royer's 1836 Log House Bed & Breakfast 90

Schussler House Bed & Breakfast......................................92

Spring View Bed & Breakfast......................................94

Stone Soup Inn 96

Story Inn 98

Sulina Farm Bed & Breakfast 100

Thorpe House Country Inn......................................102

Varns Guest House......................................104

The Victoria Bed & Breakfast......................................106

Victorian Garden Bed & Breakfast 108

The Victorian Guest House 110

Waterford Bed & Breakfast......................................112

Weaver's Country Oaks......................................114

Yoder's Zimmer mit Frühstück Haus 116

Yount's Mill Inn......................................118

Zimmer Haus Bed & Breakfast 122

Order Form 126

Index Of Inns 128

1877 House Country Inn

2408 Utica-Sellersburg Road • Jeffersonville, IN 47130
812-284-1877   888-284-1877   FAX 812-280-1877
e mail: 1877house@disknet.com
Innkeepers: Carol Pennington-Stenbro and Steve Stenbro

This 2-story historic farmhouse was built in 1877, (hence the name) and sits on top of a hill on 2 1/2 acres in a country setting. The 40' front porch, furnished with comfortable rocking chairs, and the guest rooms afford a nice view of the Louisville skyline and countryside. The gift shop is located in the summer kitchen and features local crafts and antiques. All three bedrooms have private baths, fireplaces, individual thermostats for heat or A/C, ceiling fans, and country antique furnishings. A full gourmet breakfast is served in the dining room, brick courtyard, or on the front porch. Guests may use the living room or library. Enjoy books, puzzles, games, magazines, TV, or piano. When weather allows, you may enjoy the fresh air or a game of checkers on the porch! **1877 House** is located 1 mile off the interstate and 10 minutes from Louisville, Kentucky.

Rates: $$ - $$$ Includes full breakfast. Children over age 6 are welcome. No pets or smoking, please.

BREAKFAST PUDDING (NORWEGIAN)

3 cups milk
1/2 cup cream of wheat
1/3 cup sugar

2 eggs (or substitute)
2 teaspoons almond
extract

In medium saucepan, cook milk and cream of wheat over medium heat until thick, stirring with whisk, for about 5 to 10 minutes. Add sugar and stir. Add eggs. Remove from heat and stir in almond extract until blended. Pour into dessert dishes, letting cool to lukewarm. Before refrigerating, cover with plastic wrap. Makes 6 - 8 servings.

COTTAGE PANCAKES

1 cup cottage cheese
4 eggs
1/2 cup flour

6 tablespoons melted
butter

Whip cottage cheese with mixer until smooth. Blend in eggs and flour, then mix in melted butter. Cook on non-stick griddle. Makes 3 - 4 servings.

8

EGG SCRAMBLE WITH POTATO & GREEN ONION

6 small red potatoes
6 large eggs
1/3 cup water
1/4 teaspoon salt

1/8 teaspoon pepper
1/2 cup green onions, chopped

Leave skin on potatoes and cut into chunks. Put into covered casserole and cook in microwave until just tender. Beat eggs, water, salt, and pepper. Spray large skillet with cooking spray, or melt 2 tablespoons butter, and cook potatoes until lightly browned. Add egg mixture and onions, and cook while stirring, until eggs are set. Makes 4 - 5 servings.

GERMAN PUFF PANCAKE

4 eggs
1/3 cup sugar
2 cups milk

2 cups flour
1 teaspoon salt
1 teaspoon vanilla

Beat eggs with mixer. Add sugar and milk. Add remainder of ingredients and beat until smooth. Butter a 12" skillet or 12" cake pan with thick layer of butter. Pour in batter and bake at 375° for 40 to 45 minutes, until brown and puffed up. Sprinkle with confectioner's sugar and serve hot, cut into wedges topped with fruit or syrup. Makes 6 - 8 servings.

 *Recipes From 1877 House Country Inn*

PEACH-BUTTER SYRUP

10 ounce pkg. frozen
   peaches
1/4 cup butter
1/3 cup honey
2 tablespoons lemon juice

2 teaspoons cornstarch
2 tablespoons water
1/4 teaspoon almond
   extract

Place first four ingredients in small saucepan. Cook over medium-low heat until mixture begins to boil, stirring occasionally. Mix cornstarch with water until smooth and stir into hot peaches, cooking until smooth and thickened. Remove from heat and stir in almond extract. Serve hot. Makes 4 - 5 servings.

PUMPKIN GINGERBREAD MUFFINS

3 cups sugar
1 cup vegetable oil
4 eggs
3 1/2 cups flour
2 teaspoons baking soda
1 1/2 teaspoons salt
1/2 teaspoon baking
   powder

2 teaspoons ginger
1 teaspoon cinnamon
1 teaspoon nutmeg
1 teaspoon cloves
1 teaspoon allspice
2/3 cup water
16 ounce can pumpkin

Preheat oven to 350°. Cream together sugar, oil, and eggs. Sift together flour, baking soda, salt, baking powder, and spices. Add sifted ingredients and water alternately to creamed mixture. Beat in pumpkin. Pour into greased or lined muffin pans, filling 2/3 full. Bake at 350° for 20 to 25 minutes. Makes 36 - 40 muffins.

Ahlbrand's Inn

4859 West 150 North • Greenfield, IN 46140
317-894-8839
Innkeepers: Louis and Connie Ahlbrand

Ahlbrand's Inn is a half mile off the road surrounded in 14 acres of woods. Monday through Saturday awaken to the aroma of a full country breakfast. On Sunday, breakfast includes a delightful array of homemade nut breads and muffins accompanied by fruit and coffee, tea, and juice. Five guest rooms with private bath. Enjoy the Duck Room, with twin beds; our Burgundy Room with full size bed; a queen size bed in our Bird Room, and the Hummingbird Room and Blue Room, each with a king size bed. While you're here, ease into our hot tub, relax in the sun room, play ping pong or pool in the recreation room, or simply idle away the peacefulness of the countryside in our restful country inn.

Rates: $$ - $$$ Includes full breakfast Monday through Saturday;
Nut breads & muffins, Sunday. Children are welcome. No pets,
please. Restricted smoking.

Recipes From Ahlbrand's Inn

AHLBRAND'S BANANA NUT TEA CAKE

2 cups soft oleo
3 cups sugar
7 cups flour
3 - 4 cups mashed
  bananas (or to taste)
1 1/3 cups milk
2 tablespoons baking
  powder

2 teaspoons baking
  soda
1 teaspoon cinnamon
1/2 teaspoon salt
6 eggs
2 teaspoons lemon
  juice
2 cups chopped pecans

Grease 2 angel food cake pans. Preheat oven to 350°. In large bowl, with mixer at medium speed, beat oleo with sugar until light and fluffy. Add 1 1/2 cups flour and bananas. Add remainder of flour 1 cup at a time. Add next 7 ingredients. Beat until well mixed. Constantly scrape bowl with spatula. Stir in pecans and pour into cake pans. Bake for 60 minutes. Cool and remove from pans. *Be careful and check oven. If too hot, cakes will brown too quickly. Makes 2 cakes.

AHLBRAND'S INN ARRIVAL CHEESE BALL

1 can chilled, drained,
  crushed pineapple
1 tablespoon chopped
  onion

8 ounces cream cheese,
  softened
1 tablespoon chopped
  green pepper

Be sure and drain pineapple very well or cheese ball will be too soupy. Mix all ingredients together into roll, and cover with parsley and nuts. Chill and serve with crackers.

Arbor Hill Inn

263 West Johnson Road • LaPorte, IN 46350
219-362-9200
Innkeepers: Mark Wedow, Laura Kobat, Kris Demoret

Under a canopy of majestic trees, **Arbor Hill Inn** welcomes you with gracious hospitality. Peaceful surroundings create a haven for leisure or business travel. The distinctive character of **the Inn** is revealed in four spacious suites and three well-appointed guest rooms. All rooms feature private baths as well as central air-conditioning. All suites include a romantic fireplace in bedroom, whirlpool tub, small refrigerator, and VCR. The historic Greek Revival structure was built in 1910 by William A. Jones, formerly of Chicago, as his residence, and boasts many examples of turn-of-the-century design. W. A. Jones was an ardent sportsman and student of firearms, accumulating nearly 1,000 pieces. The second largest collection in the world and the largest in the U.S., now finds its home in the LaPorte County Museum through his donation.

Rates: $$ - $$$$ Includes full breakfast on Sunday, continental breakfast during midweek. Children are welcome. No pets, please. Restricted smoking. We accept MasterCard, Visa, Am Ex, and Discover.

Recipes From Arbor Hill Inn

CHOCOLATE ZUCCHINI BREAD

3 eggs
2 cups sugar
1 cup oil
2 cups zucchini, not peeled, but put through food processor
2 squares baking chocolate, melted

3 cups flour
1 teaspoon salt
1 teaspoon baking soda
1/4 teaspoon baking powder
1 teaspoon vanilla
1 cup coarsely chopped nuts

Beat eggs until foamy. Add sugar, oil, zucchini, and melted chocolate. Mix. Add flour, salt, baking soda, baking powder, vanilla, and nuts. Bake in greased loaf pan at 350° for one hour.

STUFFED FRENCH TOAST

8 ounces cream cheese, softened
1/2 cup sugar
1 1/2 teaspoons vanilla, divided
1/2 cup chopped walnuts

16 ounce loaf French bread, cut in 1 1/2" thick slices
4 eggs
1 cup whipping cream
1/2 teaspoon ground nutmeg

Beat together cream cheese, sugar, and 1 teaspoon vanilla until fluffy. Stir in nuts and set aside. Cut bread into 10 to 12 - 1 1/2" thick slices; cut a pocket in the top of each. Fill each with 1 1/2 tablespoons of cream cheese mixture. Beat together eggs, whipping cream, 1/2 teaspoon vanilla, and nutmeg. Using tongs, dip filled bread slices into batter, being careful not to squeeze out stuffing. Cook on lightly greased griddle until golden brown. To keep slices hot for serving, place on baking sheet in warm oven. Serve with warmed syrup or warmed strawberry preserves. Makes 10 - 12 slices.

Atwater Century Farm Bed & Breakfast

4240 West U.S. 20 • LaGrange, IN 46761
219-463-2743
Innkeeper: Dianne Hostetler

The Atwater Century Farm Bed & Breakfast has three rooms. One suite with private bath and two upstairs rooms that share a bathroom. Our B&B works great for whole house rentals for families, women's groups, or church group retreats with 12 - 13 people, or 3 - 4 couples. The Bed & Breakfast is a restored family farmhouse that boasts family history, heirlooms, antique beds, quilts, and a certain charm of yesteryear. In the summer it is great to start the day with a cup of coffee and a Danish on the front porch swing. We serve a continental plus breakfast early in the morning, and you may eat at your convenience. Reservations are preferred. People are attracted to our area because of our Amish neighbors and their unique way of life. Shipshewana is just minutes away with its flea market, shops, and country restaurants.

Rates: $$ Includes continental plus breakfast. Limited accommodations for children; please ask. No pets or smoking, please.

Recipes From Atwater Century Farm B & B

CARAMEL LAYER CHOCOLATE SQUARES

14 ounce pkg. caramels
(about 50 caramels)
1/3 cup evaporated milk
1 German chocolate
   cake mix

1/3 cup evaporated milk
3/4 cup butter, melted
1 cup chopped walnuts
1 cup chocolate chips
   (6 ounces)

Combine caramels and 1/3 cup evaporated milk. Cook over low heat until melted, set aside. Grease 9" x 13" pan. Combine dry cake mix, 1/3 cup evaporated milk, melted butter, and nuts, by hand. Stir until dough holds together. Press half of dough into bottom of pan. Reserve remaining dough for topping. Bake crust at 350° for 6 minutes. Sprinkle chocolate bits over baked crust. Spread caramel mixture over chocolate. Crumble reserved dough over caramel mixture. Return to oven. Bake for 15 to 18 minutes. Cool slightly. Refrigerate to set caramel, and cut into bars. Makes 24 bars.

MONSTER COOKIES

12 eggs
4 cups brown sugar
4 cups white sugar
1 tablespoon vanilla
1 tablespoon Karo syrup
3 teaspoons baking soda
3 pounds peanut butter

1 pound butter
18 cups oatmeal (*14
   cups are in one 42
   ounce box of oatmeal)
12 ounces M&M candies
12 ounces chocolate
   chips

Mix ingredients in dishpan. Mix ingredients in order with spoon until peanut butter is mixed, then it may be easier to use hands to mix. Bake on ungreased cookie sheet at 350° for 12 to 15 minutes. Makes *lots* of cookies!

Bauer House Bed & Breakfast

4595 North Maple Grove Road • Bloomington, Indiana 47404
812-336-4383
Innkeepers: Frank and Beverly Bauer

Welcome to our 1864 red-brick country home in the rolling hills of Southern Indiana in Monroe County. **The Bauer House** boasts a double-tiered, columned porch and a spacious front yard. Surrounding the house are some of the best dry stone walls in Monroe County. There are three large rooms from which to choose. Each room is furnished with a double bed, television, air conditioner, and a rocking chair for evening relaxation. We invite our guests to a quiet, peaceful stay on a step off the beaten path.

Rates: $ Includes continental plus breakfast. Children are welcome. No pets, please. Restricted smoking.

Recipes From Bauer House Bed & Breakfast

BLUEBERRY-YOGURT MUFFINS

2 cups flour	2 tablespoons vegetable
1/3 cup sugar	oil
1 teaspoon baking powder	1 teaspoon vanilla
1 teaspoon baking soda	8 ounces vanilla yogurt
1/4 teaspoon salt	1 egg
1/4 cup unsweetened	1 cup fresh or frozen
orange juice	blueberries

Combine first five ingredients in large bowl. Make a well in center of mixture. Combine orange juice, then next four ingredients; stir well. Add to dry ingredients, stirring just until moistened. Gently fold in blueberries. Divide batter evenly among 12 muffin cups coated with cooking spray. Bake at 400° for 18 to 20 minutes until golden. Remove from pan immediately; let cool. Makes 1 dozen muffins.

CHERRY BREAKFAST CAKE

1/2 cup corn-oil	1 egg
margarine	1 teaspoon vanilla
1/2 cup yogurt or	2 cups flour
buttermilk	1 teaspoon baking
1 cup sugar	soda
1 tablespoon fresh lemon	1 - 20 ounce can
juice	cherry pie filling

Preheat oven to 350°. Spray 9" x 13" baking pan with cooking spray; set aside. In medium mixing bowl beat together margarine, yogurt, and sugar. Blend in lemon juice, egg, and vanilla. In separate bowl combine flour and baking soda, then add to liquid ingredients and mix well. Spread batter in prepared pan; then using a sharp knife score 3 lines partway through batter lengthwise, and 5 lines crosswise to make 24 squares. Spoon about 3 cherries with liquid into the center of each square. Bake for 35 minutes. Makes 2 dozen squares.

Bee Hive Bed & Breakfast

P.O. Box 1191 • Middlebury, IN 46540
219-825-5023 (FAX same)
Innkeepers: Herb and Treva Swarm

The Bee Hive Bed & Breakfast is located in the country in an Amish community. Our B&B is built with hand-sawn lumber, with open beams. An oak plank stairway leads to the loft. Locally handmade quilts are on all the beds. You may sit on the deck with iced tea and enjoy the quiet countryside. Our guests enjoy visiting and learning about our community. Oftentimes we have music with everyone singing along. Enjoy Herb's old tractors and steam engine. In the morning, wake to the smell of a country breakfast being prepared. A must is the bran muffins and fruit slush. Become one of our many return guests, and become a friend.

Rates: $$ Includes full breakfast. Children are welcome. No pets or smoking, please. We accept MasterCard and Visa.

Recipes From Bee Hive Bed & Breakfast

LEMON BARS

<u>Crust:</u>
2 cups flour
1 cup margarine

1/2 cup powdered
   sugar

<u>Filling:</u>
2 cups sugar
4 tablespoons flour
1/2 teaspoon baking
   powder

4 eggs, slightly
   beaten
1/2 cup Realemon lemon
   juice

Mix crust ingredients and press into 9" x 13" pan. Bake at 350° for 25 minutes. Mix filling ingredients in order given. Pour over baked crust and bake for 25 minutes. Cool completely and sprinkle with powdered sugar.

POPPY SEED BREAD

1 box yellow cake mix
1 teaspoon poppy seeds
1 box instant coconut
   pudding mix

4 eggs
1/2 cup oil
1 cup hot water

Combine all ingredients in mixing bowl and beat for four minutes. Pour batter into 2 greased bread loaf pans. Bake at 350° for 30 minutes. Makes 2 loaves.

The Beiger Mansion Inn

317 Lincoln Way East • Mishawaka, IN 46544
219-255-6300   800-437-0131
Innkeepers: Ron Montandon and Phil Robinson

The Beiger Mansion Inn, listed on the National Registry of Historic Places, offers elegant overnight accommodations, delightful lunches and dinner, and a fine craft gallery open to the public. **The Inn** is open year round and offers 6 rooms with private baths and one suite. Call for times and availability.

Rates: $$ - $$$$ No smoking, please. We accept all major credit cards.

Recipes From The Beiger Mansion Inn

PEACH STUFFED FRENCH TOAST

1 pound ripe peaches
(approximately 2 cups)
2 tablespoons lemon juice
1/2 cup sugar, divided
4 eggs
1 cup half and half
1/3 cup heavy cream
2 tablespoons vanilla

3/4 teaspoon cinnamon
Pinch of nutmeg
8 slices bread cut 1 1/2"
thick
4 tablespoons unsalted
butter
Maple syrup, vanilla
yogurt, or creme fraiche

Preheat oven to 375°. Blanch whole peaches in boiling water for 10 seconds, remove and place in bowl of ice water. When cool, remove, peel, and remove pits. Cut into slices. Place slices in bowl with lemon juice and 1/4 cup sugar; let stand for 30 minutes. In large shallow pan, combine eggs, half and half, cream, 1/4 cup sugar, vanilla, cinnamon, and nutmeg. Whisk until blended. Carefully cut a "pocket" at one end of each piece of bread, and stuff with peach slices. Pour excess peach juice into egg mixture, reserve extra peach slices for garnish. Soak stuffed bread in egg mixture for 4 to 5 minutes, turning once. Brown bread in pan on each side until golden brown, transfer to oven to bake for 12 minutes. Serve on warm plates with reserved peaches for garnish, and accompaniments as listed.

The Big House in the Little Woods
Bed & Breakfast

4245 South 1000 West • Millersburg, IN 46543
219-593-9076
Innkeepers: Sarah and Jacob Stoltzfus

The Big House in the Little Woods is situated along a quiet country lane in the heart of the Amish and Mennonite community. It is located in a small woods which isolates it from the surrounding countryside. The large 3,500 square foot home was newly built in 1993 - 1994 by local Mennonites, and most of the finishing work was done by Jacob and Sarah. Upon entering the house you proceed through the front foyer which features an open staircase and French doors with beveled glass. The three bedrooms are located upstairs featuring their own private bathroom. Each is uniquely decorated with both antiques and new furniture. Each room has a TV and is centrally air-conditioned. You can choose from Sarah's Room with king size bed, Susan's Room with queen size bed, or Katie's Room with full size bed.

Rates: $$ Includes full breakfast. Children over age 6 are welcome.
No pets or smoking, please. We accept MasterCard, Visa,
and Discover.

Recipes From The Big House in the Little Woods
Bed & Breakfast

CAULIFLOWER-BROCCOLI SALAD

1 head cauliflower
2 stalks broccoli
1/2 cup sliced green
onions
6 ounces Cheddar cheese,
shredded
6 ounces mozzarella
cheese

2 cups mayonnaise
1/4 cup sugar
1/2 teaspoon salt
1 tablespoon
vinegar
1 pound fried and
crumbled bacon

Cut cauliflower and broccoli into small pieces. Add to sliced onion and cheeses. Mix mayonnaise, sugar, salt, and vinegar together. Pour over vegetables and stir gently together. Add bacon last. *Can be refrigerated for 2 days. Makes 12 - 15 servings.

OLD-FASHIONED COUNTRY FRIED CORN MUSH

1 1/2 cups yellow
cornmeal
1 - 1 1/2 cups cold water
(enough to moisten
cornmeal completely)
6 cups boiling water

2 teaspoons salt
1 stick margarine or
butter, for frying
All-purpose flour, for
frying

Wet cornmeal with the cold water, until it is moistened completely. Stir into boiling water and cook for 30 minutes, stirring occasionally. Pour into 7" x 7" cake pan to cool. The mush needs to be fairly stiff. After mush is cold, slice into 1/4" slices. Roll slices in flour and fry in margarine or butter on both sides, until crisp. Serve with chipped beef or sausage gravy, syrup, or apple butter. *You may fry only a portion of the cooked mush at a time. It stores up to one week in refrigerator. Makes 16 servings.

The Book Inn Bed & Breakfast

508 West Washington • South Bend, IN 46601
219-288-1990
http://members.aol.com/bookinn/
Innkeepers: Peggy and John Livingston

Fresh flowers, antiques, 12' ceilings, and incredible butternut woodwork welcome you when you ring the bell. Elegance and attention to detail are everywhere you look, and there is even a quality used book store available for browsing anytime. One hundred year old Haviland china, sterling silver, Waterford crystal, candlelight, and other contented guests greet you at breakfast. Five bedrooms feature private baths, air conditioning, phones, and TV's. As a traveller on business in this city you will feel pampered and productive as all of your needs are met. Chicago is only an hour and a half away and over 300 antique dealers are nearby. Approved by IBBA, AAA-3 Diamond rating, and member of Professional Association of Innkeepers International. Would you like to see pictures of our rooms and connect to South Bend attractions? Visit our site on the Internet!

Rates: $$ - $$$$ Includes full gourmet breakfast. Limited availability for children. No pets or smoking, please. We accept MasterCard, Visa, Am Ex, and Discover.

Recipes From The Book Inn Bed & Breakfast

BAKED BRIE

1 wheel of Brie cheese
2 tablespoons apricot
preserves
2 tablespoons chopped
pecans

1 package Pepperidge
Farm puff pastry sheets
1 egg white

Cover top of Brie cheese wheel with apricot preserves and chopped pecans. Roll 1 sheet of puff pastry so it will fit comfortably around the Brie wheel, and overlap to seal juices. Turn wheel over so the joinings are on the bottom. Seal dough with egg white and brush top with egg white. If there is dough left, you can make leaves or another decoration for the top. Bake at 350° for 20 minutes. It should puff and brown beautifully! Surround with grapes and assorted crackers, and serve. Makes 15 servings.

PRUDY'S DIP

2 - 4 ripe avocados
1/2 cup mayonnaise
1 large carton sour
cream
1 - 1 1/2 bunches green
onions, chopped

12 ounces salsa verde
(the hotter the better!)
1 block Monterey Jack
cheese, grated
1 block Colby cheese,
grated

Mash avocados with mayonnaise. Layer ingredients in the order given in center of a large tray covered with plastic wrap (salsa will run). Make it as thick as possible. Surround the dip with nacho flavored Doritos and tortilla chips. Serves a crowd!

The Carole Lombard House

704 Rockhill Street • Fort Wayne, IN 46802
888-426-9896
Innkeepers: Bev and Dave Fiandt

The Carole Lombard House is a comfortable home adjacent to downtown Fort Wayne in the West Central Neighborhood, located on the River Greenway. It is convenient to the many good things Fort Wayne has to offer, including great restaurants, and quality cultural events - with easy highway access. **The House** has been lovingly renovated to the elegance of its time - to commemorate Carole Lombard's fame. The decor is reminiscent of the 30's and 40's. Whether you visit on business, for a getaway, to research genealogy, or to enjoy a special event, consider a stay in one of our four guest rooms. **The Carole Lombard House** serves a delicious full breakfast each morning. Selected fresh fruits are prepared immediately before serving. Gourmet coffee & tea aromas lure guests to the inviting dining room with adjoining glassed porch. Home-cooked entrees such as blueberry pancakes or strawberry blintzes, accompanying succulent Canadian bacon, are guests' favorites.

Rates: $ - $$ Includes full breakfast. Children are welcome. No pets or smoking, please. We accept MasterCard, Visa, and Discover.

Recipes From The Carole Lombard House

BEV'S BLINTZES

6 beaten eggs	1/2 - 3/4 cup straw-
1 teaspoon sugar	berries, peaches, or
3/4 teaspoon vanilla	red raspberries
2 cups milk	2 - 8 ounce pkgs. cream
2 cups flour	cheese
2 tablespoons melted	1 carton vanilla yogurt
butter	1 - 2 packets Equal (opt.)

For Blintzes: Whisk together eggs, sugar, vanilla, and milk. Add flour and melted butter. Heat frying pan to hot and spray with canola oil. Using ladle, pour in almost 1/4 cup creamy batter, and tilt pan back and forth to even out batter. Turn when top looks dry. Repeat 12 times. Cool and stack to be refrigerated, or fill for immediate serving. For Filling: Beat fruit with mixer. Add remaining ingredients and mix well. Roll 2 tablespoons filling in each blintz and place on cookie sheet. Heat rolled blintzes at 350° for 10 minutes, when all are prepared. On serving plates, place two warmed blintzes. Top with fresh fruit. A light dusting of powdered sugar and sprinkle of pecans achieves an elegant look. Add 2 or 3 slices Canadian bacon for our favorite breakfast. Makes 6 servings.

OFTEN-REQUESTED ONE-PAN PUMPKIN KRUNCH

3 cups pumpkin	1 box yellow cake mix
1 cup brown sugar	1 cup melted butter
1 cup sugar	Nutmeg, to taste
1 can evaporated milk	1/2 - 1 cup chopped
1 1/2 teaspoons cinnamon	pecans

In 9" x 13" pan, combine and spread first five ingredients. Sprinkle with dry cake mix. Drizzle with butter and dash on nutmeg, to taste. Top with pecans. Bake at 350° for 1 - 1 1/2 hours. Delicious served warm or chilled. *Appreciated as dessert for weekend breakfasts.

Cole House Bed & Breakfast

27 East Third Street • Peru, IN 46970
765-473-7636
Innkeepers: Miles and Peggy Straly

A visit to **Cole House** is like stepping back in history a hundred years. Built in 1883, by Cole Porter's grandfather, J.O. Cole. Listed on the National Register of Historic Places. Exotic hardwoods were used extensively in the home. The large downstairs rooms feature elaborate parquet floors, huge pocket doors, four unique fireplaces, beautiful chandeliers, and ornamental plaster ceilings. Guests are welcome to relax, read, or play the antique upright piano. Four large and luxurious bedrooms are available, each with its own private bath, cable TV, and air conditioning. Period furnishings are scattered throughout the home.

Rates: $ - $$ Includes full breakfast. Children are welcome. No pets or smoking, please. We accept MasterCard, Visa, Am Ex, and Discover.

Recipes From Cole House Bed & Breakfast

CHICKEN & RICE BAKE

1 can cream of mushroom soup	1/4 teaspoon all-seasoning salt
1 cup water	1/4 teaspoon pepper
3/4 cup long-grain rice	1/4 teaspoon paprika
1/2 cup chopped peppers	4 boneless, skinless chicken breast halves

In 2-quart shallow baking dish mix soup, water, rice, peppers, all-seasoning salt, pepper, and paprika. Place chicken on rice mixture. Sprinkle with additional paprika, pepper, and all-seasoning salt. Cover. Bake at 375° for 45 minutes or until done. Makes 4 servings.

MUSHROOM SCRAMBLED EGGS

6 eggs	1 teaspoon sugar
1/2 cup cream of mushroom soup	Dash of soy sauce
1/4 cup milk or water	Dash of pepper

Mix all ingredients together in bowl. Pour into warm skillet. Stir and scramble eggs until done. Makes 3 servings.

The Country Victorian Bed & Breakfast

435 South Main Street • Middlebury, IN 46540
219-825-2568
Innkeepers: Mark and Becky Potterbaum

"A Delightful Step Back in Time" - This 100 year old Victorian home, turned B&B, charms guests with intricate architectural detail, comfortable refreshing decor, and warm hospitality. The Amish influence pervades the inn with the pleasant cadence of horse and buggies. Waking to that rhythmic sound complemented by the aroma of freshly baked goodies, and the comfort of a good night's sleep, gives one the pleasure of an extra special old-fashioned retreat. "It's like one long hug" - one guest shared. Five guest rooms with private baths (one with 2-person jacuzzi) make it easy to accommodate up to twelve guests comfortably. A full, hot breakfast is served in the dining room on Grandmother's china. And if guests are able to check-in between 4:00 and 6:00 P.M. they are invited to enjoy "afternoon tea" - little cookies, coffee, and an assortment of teas.

Rates: $$ - $$$ Includes full breakfast. Children are welcome. No pets or smoking, please. We accept MasterCard, Visa, and Discover.

Recipes From The Country Victorian B & B

CHOCK FULL O' CHUNKS AFTERNOON TEA COOKIES

2 cups butter	1 teaspoon salt
2 cups brown sugar	1 teaspoon baking powder
2 cups white sugar	2 teaspoons baking soda
4 eggs	Your choice of goodies:
2 teaspoons vanilla	Semi-sweet chocolate
5 cups oatmeal (measure,	chips, toffee bits, white
then blend into powder)	chocolate chunks, pecan
4 cups flour	pieces, macadamia nuts

Cream butter and sugars. Add eggs and vanilla. Blend oatmeal into powder and mix separately with flour, salt, baking powder, and baking soda. Add to butter mixture. Add your choice of goodies, as few or as many as you like; be creative! Chill dough. Roll into balls. Bake on ungreased cookie sheets at 375° for 9 minutes. Dough can be refrigerated for later use. Makes a huge amount of cookies!

SAUSAGE APPLE QUICHE

Pie Crust:

3 cups flour	1 teaspoon salt
4 tablespoons sugar	1 cup oil
	1 tablespoon milk

Filling:

1 pound browned country sausage (plus 1 tablespoon fresh or dried thyme)	13 eggs
	1 1/2 pints half and half
	Salt and pepper, to taste
1 finely chopped tart apple, unpeeled	1 cup grated Cheddar cheese

Mix pie crust ingredients with fork and press into 2 pie pans. Mix together all filling ingredients. Pour into pie shells and bake at 350° for one hour. *Can be poured into shells and refrigerated overnight. Bring to room temperature for 10 minutes before baking. Makes 2 deep dish quiches or 12 large slices.

Dunes Shore Inn Bed & Breakfast

33 Lakeshore County Road • Beverly Shores, IN 46301-0807
219-879-9029
Innkeepers: Rosemary and Fred Braun

A casual B&B in secluded Beverly Shores, surrounded by the Indiana Dunes National Lakeshore. We are one block from Lake Michigan, one hour from Chicago, and 3 hours from Indianapolis. Whether a party of one, or a group, this is the ideal place to relax in a four-season oasis - miles of wooded trails and beaches await. Easy access to national and state park, marina, shopping, restaurants. **The Inn** has 12 comfortable guest rooms on upper two floors - each floor with its own small lounge. In summer enjoy patio, screen house, picnic area with grill. **Inn** guests have use of a refrigerator. A special continental breakfast, varying with the season, is served in the ground floor common room. Shared bathrooms.

Rates: $ - $$$ Includes continental plus breakfast. Children are welcome. No pets or smoking, please.

GESUNDHEITS KUCHEN (POUND CAKE)

1 1/2 cups sugar	4 eggs
1/2 teaspoon salt	1/2 cup milk
1 teaspoon vanilla	2 cups flour
1/2 pound butter	Powdered sugar

Add sugar, salt, and vanilla to softened and creamed butter. Beat in eggs and milk. Slowly add flour; mix well. Pour batter into well-greased fluted cylindrical pan (Gugelhupf pan). Bake at 350° for 60 to 70 minutes. After cake is removed from pan, allow to cool. Dust with powdered sugar.

PALATSCHINKEN

3 tablespoons sugar	1 cup milk
Pinch of salt	1/2 cup half and half
1 cup flour	2 tablespoons butter,
3 eggs	melted

Add sugar and salt to flour. Beat in eggs until batter is smooth. Add milk, and half and half while beating. Allow batter to rest at least 30 minutes. Batter should be fairly thin. Heat pan, melt butter; add batter. Tilt pan to spread batter. Brown lightly on one side. Turn with spatula and brown other side. Serve with sugar/cinnamon mixture or fill with fruit, jam, chopped ham, etc. as desired. Roll up. Serve hot with whipped cream or sour cream. Makes 4 servings.

Empty Nest Bed & Breakfast

13347 County Road 12 • Middlebury, IN 46540
219-825-1042
Innkeepers: Sherry and Tim Bryant

Four-level traditional home on a hillside overlooking two ponds - home to swans, geese, and ducks - gentle hills, woods, and flowered fields. Tim and Sherry are pleased to help you find the fun things to do - antique and craft gift shops, Shipshewana's famous 1,000 stall flea market and auction, Amish country, museums, parks, rivers and lakes, Goshen College and Notre Dame University - to entertain on the grand piano, and cook up a special hearty breakfast to remember. Refresh yourself in the secluded outdoor swimming pool. Guest rooms are newly furnished, including queen size beds, and at least one antique! Air conditioned. The kids have "flown the nest," so we are glad to attend to your needs, in this country setting.

Rates: $$ - $$$ Includes full breakfast. Children over age 12 are welcome. No pets or smoking, please. We accept MasterCard, Visa, and Discover.

Recipes From Empty Nest Bed & Breakfast

APPLE-CINNAMON BAKED FRENCH TOAST

1 large loaf French bread,
  cut 1 1/2" thick
8 extra large eggs,
  slightly beaten
1 cup sugar, divided
3 1/2 cups milk

1 tablespoon vanilla
6 - 8 medium cooking
  apples, sliced
1 tablespoon cinnamon
1 teaspoon nutmeg
2 tablespoons butter

Slice bread into 1 1/2" thick slices. Spray 9" x 13" glass baking dish with cooking spray. Place bread in pan, side by side, tightly. Beat together eggs, 1/2 cup sugar, milk, and vanilla for about 30 seconds. Pour half of mixture over bread. Peel, core, and slice apples. Place apples on top of bread. Pour remainder of egg mixture evenly over apples. Mix remaining 1/2 cup sugar with spices. Sprinkle evenly over apples. Dot surface with bits of butter. Cover and refrigerate overnight. Next morning, remove cover. Preheat oven to 350°. Bake for one hour. Remove from oven; let stand 5 to 10 minutes. Slice. Serve with heated maple syrup. Makes 10 - 12 servings.

SHERRY'S BRUNCH EGGS

2 cups frozen hash brown
  potatoes
1 cup shredded Cheddar
  cheese
2 tablespoons onion,
  diced
1/2 - 10 ounce pkg.
  smoked sausage links,
  sliced (5 ounces)

4 ounce can sliced
  mushrooms, drained
4 eggs, slightly beaten
3 tablespoons milk
1/2 teaspoon salt
1/8 teaspoon black
  pepper
1/4 cup shredded Cheddar
  cheese

Layer ingredients into 9" square glass baking dish as follows: Potatoes, 1 cup shredded cheese, onions, sausage slices, and mushrooms. Mix eggs, milk, salt, and pepper. Pour over ingredients in baking dish. Top with 1/4 cup shredded cheese. Chill overnight covered. Remove cover. Bake at 350° for 30 to 35 minutes. Makes 4 - 6 servings. *Double ingredients for 9" x 13" baking dish for 8 - 12 servings.

The Folke Family Farm Inn

18406 Pribble Road • Lawrenceburg, IN 47025
812-537-7025   888-593-6358
Innkeeper: JoAnn Folke

The Folke Family Farm Inn is a 14 room farmhouse, in the Folke Family since 1883 and designated by the Indiana Department of Commerce as an "Historic Hoosier Homestead". Two bedrooms with private baths, and a two bedroom suite with private bath and sitting area. Glassed-in enclosed solarium with panoramic views. Complimentary full breakfast is served to guests. Offering a quiet, relaxed atmosphere, away from the hustle and bustle, and a walking trail with panoramic views of the Tri-State area of Indiana, Kentucky and Ohio. While walking you may see rabbits, wild turkeys, coyotes, deer, and many species of birds. Located in scenic SE Indiana just outside Lawrenceburg and approximately 30 minutes from downtown Cincinnati, Ohio. Convenient to I-74, I-275, and US 50. Minutes to Greater Cincinnati/Northern Kentucky International Airport, Ohio River, Gaming Riverboats, Public Boat Dock, winter skiing, and area unique shops. Within two miles of medical services.

Rates: $ Includes full breakfast. Children are welcome. No pets, please. Restricted smoking. We accept MasterCard and Visa.

Recipes From The Folke Family Farm Inn

EGG CASSEROLE

1 pound mild bulk
sausage, browned
8 eggs
1/2 cup milk
1/2 teaspoon prepared
mustard

1/4 teaspoon salt
Sprinkle of black pepper
2 cups thawed hash
brown potatoes
1 cup shredded mild
Cheddar cheese

Brown sausage in skillet on stove. Drain and set aside. Beat eggs, milk, mustard, salt, and pepper until well mixed. Add drained sausage, hash brown potatoes, and Cheddar cheese. Pour into 9" x 13" casserole sprayed with Pam. Refrigerate overnight. Heat oven to 350°; bake for 45 minutes. *Leftovers can be reheated in microwave.

YEAST BISCUITS

1 1/3 cups milk
1/4 cup sugar

1 pkg. rapid rise yeast
4 cups Bisquick mix

Heat milk and sugar in microwave to 115°. Stir in yeast. Mix well. Mix in Bisquick until well mixed. Knead dough on cloth covered pastry board that is sprinkled with Bisquick for 5 minutes. Add additional Bisquick until batter is no longer sticky. Cover with mixing bowl for 15 minutes. Roll out dough and cut with biscuit cutter. Place biscuits on lightly greased pizza pan, cover with foil, and refrigerate overnight. Heat oven to 400° and bake for 20 minutes or until done. After removing from oven, brush with butter and sprinkle with sugar.

The Frederick-Talbott Inn

13805 Allisonville Road • Fishers, IN 46038
317-578-3600
Innkeepers: Susan Muller and Ann Irvine

Eleven individually styled rooms with private baths exude the luxury and comfort once reserved for a less hurried time. Tastefully appointed in nineteenth century antiques, the establishment is a reflection of the innkeepers' gracious hospitality. So unlike a hotel is the ambience beyond the main entry that one quickly forgets even having signed the registry. The home of Indiana's finest small meeting facility for up to 24 people.

Rates: $$$$ Includes full breakfast. Restricted smoking. We accept MasterCard, Visa, Am Ex, and Discover.

Recipes From The Frederick-Talbott Inn

CHOCOLATE RASPBERRY STRATA

4 cups cubed Hawaiian
 bread
3/4 cup semi-sweet
 chocolate chips
1/2 pint fresh red
 raspberries
4 eggs

1/2 cup milk
1/2 cup whipping cream
1 teaspoon vanilla
1/4 cup sugar
Whipped cream for
 garnish (opt.)

Place bread cubes evenly in sprayed 11" x 7" baking dish. Sprinkle with chocolate chips and 2/3 of the raspberries. In medium bowl, whisk together eggs, milk, cream, vanilla, and sugar until well-blended. Pour evenly over bread mixture. Cover with plastic wrap and refrigerate overnight. Preheat oven to 325°. Bake for 35 to 40 minutes. Let stand for 10 to 20 minutes. Serve warm garnished with remaining raspberries and whipped cream. Makes 10 - 15 servings.

SHERRIED EGG CASSEROLE

3 dozen eggs
1 1/3 cups milk
2 cans cream of
 mushroom soup
1/4 cup sherry

2 - 4 ounce cans sliced
 mushrooms, drained
1/2 pound grated Cheddar
 cheese

Beat eggs and milk together. Scramble egg mixture until soft. Place a layer of eggs in 9" x 13" Pyrex dish. Mix together mushroom soup and sherry. Fold in sliced mushrooms. Layer mushroom mixture on top of cooked egg mixture. Top with grated cheese. Cover and refrigerate overnight. Place in COLD oven; set at 250° and bake for one and one-half hours. Makes 12 - 20 servings.

Gray Goose Inn

350 Indian Boundary Road • Chesterton, IN 46304
219-926-5781
Innkeepers: Tim Wilk and Chuck Ramsey

Gray Goose Inn, is located in the heart of "Dunes Country", situated on 100 wooded acres, overlooking tranquil Lake Palomara. Featuring traditional English decor, four poster beds, suites with fireplaces and jacuzzi. Eight rooms, most with lake view. Private baths, in-room phones, and TV's. Gourmet breakfast. Wedding and honeymoon packages, meeting and special event rooms, gift certificates. Featured in <u>Country Inns</u> and <u>Glamour</u> magazines. <u>American Ways</u> (an American Airlines magazine) says "An elegant, antique-filled English style hostelry, 'A Flight of Fancy'."

Rates: $$$$ Includes full breakfast. Children over age 12 are welcome. No pets, please. Restricted smoking. We accept MasterCard, Visa, Am Ex, and Discover.

Recipes From Gray Goose Inn

BAKED EGGS WITH SOUR CREAM

1 3/4 cups sour cream
1/4 cup melted butter
(1/2 stick)
1/2 cup bread crumbs

6 eggs
1/3 cup grated Cheddar
or Swiss cheese

Butter shallow casserole. Put in 1 1/4 cups sour cream and half of the melted butter. With back of spoon make six depressions; sprinkle with half of bread crumbs. Break eggs, one at a time, into a cup and carefully slip one egg into each depression. Mix remaining sour cream and melted butter together and spoon over eggs. Sprinkle with remaining crumbs and top with grated cheese. Bake at 325° for 20 to 25 minutes or until eggs are set. Makes 6 servings. *Recipe can be doubled.

BREAKFAST/BRUNCH COFFEE CAKE RING

4 tablespoons butter
(1/2 stick)
4 tablespoons brown
sugar
15 maraschino cherries

1/2 cup chopped nuts
1/2 cup sugar
1 teaspoon cinnamon
2 cups Bisquick
2/3 cup milk

Preheat oven to 400°. Melt butter. Put 2 tablespoons in bottom of 9" ring mold. Sprinkle in brown sugar, cherries, and all but 3 tablespoons chopped nuts. In small bowl, mix 3 tablespoons chopped nuts, sugar, and cinnamon. In another bowl, add Bisquick, and stir in milk with a fork. Beat about 15 to 20 times. Mixture should be stiff and sticky, shape dough into 12 balls. Roll each ball into the rest of melted butter; then roll into cinnamon/nut mixture. Put balls into ring mold. Bake for 25 to 30 minutes. When done, turn upside down onto a plate. Serve warm. Makes 12 servings.

42

CHRISTMAS BUBBLES

2 packages dry yeast
1/4 cup warm water
4 sticks (1 pound)
  butter

1 cup sugar
1 egg
4 1/2 cups flour
Colored sugar

Dissolve yeast in warm water. Cream butter; add sugar, and egg; beat until light and fluffy. Blend in yeast, then blend in flour. Mix well. Shape into small balls and dip into colored sugar. Bake at 375° on greased cookie sheet for 10 to 12 minutes. Makes 24 to 36 rolls.

EASY AND QUICK CORN BREAD PUDDING

2 - 15 ounce cans whole
  kernel corn, drained
2 - 15 ounce cans
  creamed corn

2 boxes Jiffy corn bread
  mix
1/2 pound melted butter
  (2 sticks)

Mix all ingredients together. Pour into greased 9" x 13" pan. Bake at 350° for one hour. Makes 10 servings.

Recipes From Gray Goose Inn

EASY BUTTERY POUND CAKE

2 sticks butter (1/2 pound)
8 ounces cream cheese
1 1/2 cups sugar
4 eggs
1 1/2 teaspoons vanilla
1 3/4 cups sifted flour
1 1/2 teaspoons baking powder

Combine butter and cream cheese. Beat until creamy. Add sugar, beat 5 minutes. Add eggs one at a time, beating well after each addition. Add vanilla. Mix in flour and baking powder. Pour into greased and floured bundt pan. Bake at 350° for one hour. Makes 8 - 10 servings.

SOUTH OF THE BORDER EGG BAKE

10 - 12 eggs, lightly beaten
1/2 cup flour
1 teaspoon baking powder
1/2 teaspoon salt
1 1/2 pints small curd cottage cheese
1/4 pound butter, melted
1 pound Monterey Jack cheese, grated
4 ounces diced & seeded green chilies (hot or mild, per taste)
1/4 cup chopped red pimiento
Small can drained whole kernel corn (opt.)

Preheat oven to 350°. Beat eggs until light. Add remaining ingredients. Mix very well. Pour into buttered 9" x 13" baking dish. Bake for about 35 minutes or until brown and puffy. Serve while hot. Makes 10 - 12 servings.

Hill Top Country Inn

1733 County Road 28 • Auburn, IN 46706
219-281-2298
Innkeepers: Charles and Becky Derrow

Hill Top Inn is an historic farm home, a former tourist farm house from 1925 to the 1940's. Bed chambers (3) and sitting rooms are decorated with quilts, antiques, and stenciling. The kitchen boasts of hand-crafted pine cupboards, an antique dough table, an original Nappanee cupboard, and a cast-iron stove. Breakfast is served in the country dining room with colonnades and stained glass-doored cupboards. Summer walking through the woods, winter cross country skiing, and relaxing on farm porches provide for your fun. Many antique and craft shops, Auburn Cord Duesenberg Museum, and a state park are near.

Rates: $$ - $$$ Includes full breakfast. No pets or smoking, please.

Recipes From Hill Top Country Inn

BECKY'S APPLE PANCAKES

1 cup unbleached flour	1 tablespoon vegetable
1 tablespoon sugar	oil
1/2 teaspoon salt	5 medium apples, peeled
1 egg	& thinly sliced
1 cup 2% milk	Confectioner's sugar

In bowl, combine flour, sugar, and salt. In another bowl lightly beat egg; add milk and oil. Add dry ingredients and stir until smooth. Fold in apples. Pour batter by 1/2 cupfuls onto lightly greased hot griddle and spread to form a 5" circle. Turn when bubbles form. Cook second side until golden brown and apples are tender. Sprinkle with confectioner's sugar. Makes 14 - 16 pancakes.

HILL TOP'S BREAKFAST CRESCENTS

1 tube refrigerated	1 package brown 'n'
crescent rolls	serve sausages for
Cherry or apricot	filling
preserves for filling	

About 20 minutes before serving, unroll and separate crescent rolls from tube. Filling Choice #1: Spoon 1/2 tablespoon either cherry or apricot preserves into center of each crescent roll. Roll and seal edges. Bake as label directs. Filling Choice #2: Cook brown 'n' serve sausages as directed. Place one on each crescent roll; seal edges tightly. Bake until browned. Makes 8 servings.

The Hutchinson Mansion Inn

220 West Tenth Street • Michigan City, IN 46360
219-879-1700
Innkeepers: Ben and Mary DuVal

A stay at the **Hutchinson Mansion** evokes the leisured elegance of a more gracious era. Built in 1875, this historic structure has been restored to its former grandeur and furnished with fine antiques. Beautiful stained glass windows, high beamed and decorated ceilings abound. Wander about **the Mansion** exploring its nooks and crannies, lounge in the parlor and library, relax in its gardens, or enjoy a game of croquet on the east lawn. Each of 10 rooms and suites has its own distinctive character: the romance of the Patterson Room with its 1820's southern plantation bed; the country charm of the Servant's Quarters with its white and gold iron bed, private porch, and original bath; the privacy and spaciousness of the Carriage House luxury suites. Located in Michigan City's historic district, less than a mile from the shores of Lake Michigan, minutes from the National Lakeshore and Indiana Dunes State Park.

Rates: $$ - $$$$ Includes full breakfast. Young children are strongly discouraged. No pets, please. Restricted smoking. We accept MasterCard, Visa, and Am Ex.

Recipes From The Hutchinson Mansion Inn

FORGIVING BEEF STROGANOFF

1/4 cup butter
3/4 cup minced onions
2 pounds beef, cut into
  thin strips
1 clove garlic, minced
3 tablespoons flour
1 1/2 teaspoons salt
1/4 teaspoon pepper

1/4 teaspoon paprika
  (opt.)
1/2 pound fresh mush-
  rooms, sliced (or 4
  ounce can mushrooms)
1 can undiluted cream of
  mushroom soup
1 cup sour cream

In large skillet, sauté onions in butter until golden. Add beef, garlic, flour, salt, pepper, and paprika (if desired), and cook until meat is browned. Turn down heat and add mushrooms and soup. Simmer about 10 minutes. Stir in sour cream. Serve over cooked rice. *This recipe is very forgiving and doesn't tend to curdle.

ORANGE NUT MUFFINS

2 large oranges
2 eggs
1/2 cup sugar
1/2 cup butter, melted
2 cups flour

2 teaspoons baking
  powder
1/2 teaspoon baking soda
1/2 teaspoon salt
1/2 cup chopped walnuts

Preheat oven to 400°. Grease muffin tins. Using grater or small paring knife, remove zest from oranges. Trim off and discard pith and membrane, retaining just the flesh sections of orange. Chop orange and zest together using a chopper, or processor, or by hand. This should amount to approximately one cup. In large bowl whisk eggs. Add sugar, and melted butter, and stir well. In separate bowl combine flour, baking powder, baking soda, and salt, and blend. Add chopped oranges, then flour mixture, to egg mixture and stir until blended. Stir in nuts. Fill muffin tins 1/2 to 2/3 full. Bake for 15 minutes or until tester comes out clean. Serve hot. Makes 14 - 16 muffins.

Indian Creek Bed & Breakfast

20300 County Road 18 • Goshen, IN 46528
219-875-6606 FAX 219-875-3968
Innkeepers: Herman and Shirley Hochstetler

Our new Victorian style home is filled with family antiques and collectibles and has been lovingly decorated throughout. The guest rooms, named after our grandchildren, have either queen or full size beds, private baths, and each is uniquely different from the next. Our 42' dining room, kitchen, and great room combination is light and airy with it's 18' high ceiling. The open stairway to the lower level reveals a family room, game room with a pin ball machine, TV, and a table for card playing or putting a puzzle together. Enjoy our deck to watch for deer, or stroll to the woods on our 96 acres.

Rates: $$$ Includes full breakfast. Children are welcome. No pets, please. Restricted smoking. We accept MasterCard, Visa, Am Ex, and Discover.

Recipes From Indian Creek Bed & Breakfast

OVERNIGHT PECAN FRENCH TOAST

4 eggs
2/3 cup orange
  juice
1/3 cup milk
1/4 cup sugar
1/4 teaspoon ground
  nutmeg

1/2 teaspoon vanilla
  extract
8 ounce loaf Italian
  bread, cut into 1" slices
1/3 cup butter or
  margarine, melted
1/2 cup pecan pieces

With wire whisk beat together eggs, orange juice, milk, sugar, nutmeg, and vanilla. Place bread in single layer in casserole that just fits the slices. Pour milk mixture over bread. Cover and refrigerate overnight, turning once. Pour melted butter on a jelly roll pan, spreading evenly. Arrange soaked bread slices in a single layer. Sprinkle with pecans. Bake at 400° until golden, 20 to 25 minutes. Serve with maple syrup and butter, if desired. Makes 4 servings.

STRAWBERRY-GLAZED FRUIT SALAD

1 quart fresh straw-
  berries, halved
1 - 20 ounce can pine-
  apple chunks, drained

4 firm bananas, sliced
1 jar or pouch (16
  ounces) strawberry
  glaze

In large bowl, gently toss strawberries, pineapple, and bananas; fold in the glaze. Chill for one hour. Makes 6 - 8 servings. *Strawberry glaze can often be found in the produce section of your grocery store.

The Inn at Aberdeen

3158 South State Road 2 • Valparaiso, IN 46383
219-465-3753
Innkeeper: Sharron Simon

The unique design of **The Inn** and the experience of our staff allow us to meet a variety of needs, from a simple room for an evening to an elaborate affair for many. **The Inn** offers eleven guest suites. Eight have king beds and three have two queen beds, with an additional rollaway bed per floor. Fireplaces, jacuzzis, luxurious robes, fine linens, towels, and a whole host of personal amenities await our guests. An evening snack, free beverages, hot and cold, and a full gourmet breakfast complement your stay. The St. Andrews Conference Center provides executive class surroundings for that special meeting, presentation, or retreat, with audiovisual support provided. You can book the entire **Inn** for that special getaway, to remember old times, or to plan for the future. Spend a weekend with us sleuthing for clues among our other guests to determine "who done it" on our Mystery Weekends.

Rates: $$$ - $$$$ Includes full breakfast. Children welcome. No pets or smoking, please. We accept MasterCard, Visa, Am Ex, Discover, and Diners.

Recipes From The Inn at Aberdeen

CORN CHOWDER

1 pound bacon, fried
1 large onion, chopped
4 stalks celery, chopped
3 medium carrots,
  chopped
3 - 4 medium potatoes,
  chopped
Water to cover

3 regular size cans
  creamed corn
2 quarts half and half or
  cream
Salt and pepper, to taste
3 - 4 tablespoons potato
  flakes or buds (if
  needed)

Brown bacon and remove from drippings. Sauté chopped onion, celery, carrots, and potatoes in bacon drippings. Add enough water to cover; simmer until tender. Add corn. Crumble bacon and add to chowder. Add half and half until desired thickness. May add potato flakes or buds to thicken, if necessary. Serve with one pat of butter on top, with croutons and/or chives. Makes 16 servings.

SHARRON'S BAKED EGGS

12 eggs
1 cup diced mushrooms
1 cup diced onion
1 cup green chilies,
  chopped
1 cup chopped broccoli
  (opt.)
2 cups diced ham or
  cooked sausage

1 pint sour cream
2 cups shredded cheese
  (Cheddar alone or
  mixed with Monterey
  Jack)
Black olives & roasted
  red peppers for garnish
2 cups salsa on the
  side

Beat eggs until fluffy; add mushrooms, onions, green chilies, and broccoli (if desired). Scramble eggs until done and pour into 9" x 13" baking dish. Top with diced ham or sausage. Layer sour cream and finally top with cheese. Decorate with black olives and roasted red peppers. Bake at 350° for one hour. Serve with salsa on the side. Makes 12 servings. *May add diced potatoes. Do not scramble but mix first five ingredients together; pour into dish. Layer remainder of ingredients. Bake at 350° for one hour and 15 minutes.

Inn at Bethlehem

Walnut & Riverview • Bethlehem, Indiana 47104
812-293-3975
Innkeepers: Chester and Jeanne Browne

A stately inn and lodge rest on twenty six acres rolling gently to the Ohio River, in a secluded valley in Southern Indiana. We are halfway between historic Madison, Indiana and Louisville, Kentucky. Peace and tranquility are the order of the day. Rocking chairs, hammocks, and bicycles are some of the choices with hiking, fishing, or antiquing for the more adventurous. A boat dock is available for overnight guests. Furnished with many period antiques, and all ten bedrooms have private, tiled baths and air- conditioning. We are a special place for a weekend away, a business or church retreat, wedding reception, or family get-together. Breakfasts feature fresh fruit compote, homemade muffins, and specialties such as quiche or cheese stratas.

Rates: $$ - $$$$ Includes full breakfast. Children over age 12 are welcome. No pets or smoking, please.

Recipes From Inn at Bethlehem

BAKED SALMON WITH SUMMER SAUCE

6 - 4 ounce salmon
fillets
1/4 cup melted butter
Salt & pepper, to taste
Juice of one lemon
1/2 teaspoon minced
garlic

1/4 cup Chardonnay
1 cup seeded, diced
tomatoes (red & yellow)
2 tablespoons snipped
chives
1 tablespoon chopped,
fresh basil

Spray 9" x 13" x 2" baking pan with vegetable spray. Arrange salmon fillets in pan. Divide butter among fillets. Season with salt, and pepper. Sprinkle lemon juice over all. Bake uncovered at 350° for 8 to 10 minutes or until done (depends on thickness of fillets). Remove fillets from pan and keep warm. Pour pan drippings into medium sauté pan. Add garlic and Chardonnay. Simmer for 2 minutes; add remainder of ingredients and simmer for 2 more minutes. Arrange salmon on plates and spoon sauce over top. Makes 6 servings.
*Chicken breasts are great like this, too!

DEVILED WALLEYE

1 minced shallot
1/2 small red bell pepper,
finely diced
1/4 pound butter
Juice of one lemon
1 tablespoon Creole
mustard (or dijon)
1/4 teaspoon garlic
powder
Dash of Tabasco sauce
(or to taste)

1 teaspoon tamari (or
soy sauce)
1/2 cup fresh sourdough
bread crumbs
1/2 cup grated Swiss
cheese
1 teaspoon chopped
parsley
Salt & pepper, to taste
2 pounds walleye
fillets

Sauté shallot and red pepper in butter until soft. Remove from heat and add remainder of ingredients except salt, pepper, and walleye - tossing well to combine. Salt and pepper walleye fillets. Cover evenly with crumb mixture. Bake at 350° for 15 minutes or until fish flakes easily. Makes 4 - 6 servings.

FALL FLAVORS QUICHE

1 deep-dish pie crust to
  fit 9" - 9 1/2" pie pan
1 cup whipping cream
4 eggs
1 tablespoon all-purpose
  flour
Salt & pepper, to taste
2 Granny Smith apples,
  peeled & cored,
  sliced thinly

3/4 cup grated sharp
  Cheddar cheese
3/4 cup grated Swiss
  cheese
1/2 pound sage flavored
  breakfast sausage,
  cooked, drained &
  crumbled

Roll out pie crust; pat into pan, and flute edges. Prick bottom and sides with fork. Bake at 425° for 8 minutes. Remove crust. Reduce oven temperature to 350°. Whip together cream, eggs, flour, salt, and pepper. Fold in apples, cheeses, and cooked sausage. Pour into prepared crust and bake for 50 to 60 minutes or until filling is set. Let rest 10 minutes before serving. Makes 6 - 8 servings.

FARMERS CHEESE DIP

1 cup 4% cottage cheese
1/2 cup mayonnaise
1/4 cup sour cream
2 teaspoons chopped,
  fresh parsley
1 teaspoon chopped,
  fresh dill
Dash of Tabasco sauce

1 clove garlic, mashed
  to paste
1/2 teaspoon seasoned
  salt
1 teaspoon chives,
  chopped
1 teaspoon Worcester-
  shire sauce

Mix all ingredients together well in medium bowl. Cover and refrigerate overnight. Serve with assorted fresh vegetables. Snow peas are very good with this dip. Makes 2 cups.

Recipes From Inn at Bethlehem

MACQUE CHOUX

4 cups sweet corn, cut
from the cob (scrape
knife down cob to
release milk from corn)
1 small onion, diced
1/4 cup diced red
pepper
2 tablespoons butter
1/2 teaspoon salt

1/4 teaspoon freshly
ground black pepper
(or to taste)
1 teaspoon sugar
1 tablespoon chopped
parsley
1 tablespoon chopped
chives
1/4 cup half & half

Sauté onion and red pepper in butter over medium heat until onion starts to turn clear. Add corn, salt, pepper and sugar. Cook on low heat for 30 minutes. If corn is too thick, add small amount of water. Remove from heat and add parsley, chives, and half & half. Serve. Makes 6 - 8 servings.

WILD MUSHROOM & SHALLOT MUFFINS

2 cups unbleached all-
purpose flour
1 tablespoon sugar
1 tablespoon baking
powder
3/4 teaspoon salt
1/4 teaspoon freshly
ground black pepper

1/3 cup butter, melted
1 egg, beaten
1 cup whole milk
1 1/2 cups chopped, fresh
morels (or shiitake or
portabella or a mixture)
1 large or 2 small
shallots, minced

Sift first four ingredients. Add pepper. Stir in melted butter, egg, and milk just until moist. Fold in mushrooms (be sure and wash them well), and shallots. Spray muffin cups with cooking spray and fill. Bake at 400° for 20 minutes. Makes 12 muffins.

Kati-Scarlett Bed & Breakfast

1037 North Main, P.O. Box 756 • Lapel, IN 46051
765-534-4937
Innkeepers: Charles and Sharon Wilson-Dopirak

The Kati-Scarlett B&B is a lovely red brick 1928 American Four-Square-style house, nestled in the heart of Lapel. The B&B is situated on North Main Street where you can relax on the shaded front porch while enjoying the serenity of this quiet country community. The stress and strains are suspended the moment you wander to the gazebo in the bricked, walled-in back yard, or rest in one of the three guest rooms (shared bath) reflecting the silver screen's greatest love story. Whether you stay at the **Kati-Scarlett** in summer, savoring the garden, or in winter, while snuggling to the warmth of the wood-burning fireplace, your thoughts will wander back to a time of power, passion, and romance -- a time that's gone with the wind.

Rates: $$ Includes continental plus breakfast. Children are welcome. No pets, please. Restricted smoking.

Recipes From Kati-Scarlett Bed & Breakfast

APPLE-BERRY BREAKFAST CRISP

Topping:
1 cup quick or old-fashioned oatmeal, uncooked
1/2 cup firmly packed brown sugar

1/3 cup margarine or butter, melted
2 tablespoons all-purpose flour

Filling:
4 cups thinly sliced & peeled apples (4 med.)
2 cups frozen blueberries or sliced strawberries
1/4 cup firmly packed brown sugar

1/4 cup frozen orange juice concentrate, thawed
2 tablespoons all-purpose flour
1 teaspoon ground cinnamon

Heat oven to 350°. In medium bowl, combine topping ingredients, set aside. In large bowl, combine filling ingredients; stir until fruit is evenly coated. Spoon filling into 8" square glass baking dish. Sprinkle topping evenly over fruit. Bake for 30 to 35 minutes or until apples are tender. Serve warm with yogurt, if desired.

SAUSAGE BREAKFAST CASSEROLE

1 package frozen hash brown potatoes
1 pound sausage, cooked and crumbled
1 onion, chopped

1 cup grated cheese
8 eggs
1 tablespoon milk
1/2 teaspoon salt
1/2 teaspoon pepper

Brown sausage and chopped onion together. Drain and crumble. Spray 9" x 13" glass baking dish with Pam. Layer hash browns, cooked sausage, and cheese. Beat eggs and milk. Add salt, and pepper. Pour eggs over mixture in baking dish. Bake at 350° for 25 to 35 minutes, or until inserted knife comes out clean. Makes 6 - 8 servings.

Lanning House & 1920's Annex

206 E. Poplar Street • Salem, IN 47167
812-883-3484
Innkeeper: Jeanette Hart

The Lanning House (1873) and the **1920 Annex** are a part of the Salem Museum area called the John Hay Center. Hay was Lincoln's secretary. Salem is 45 minutes from Louisville, Kentucky, and near Madison Spring Mill Park and Corydon's state capitol. Great for genealogical researchers, history lovers, and antique buffs. Seven rooms available.

Rates: $ - $$ Includes full breakfast. No pets or smoking, please.

Recipes From Lanning House & 1920's Annex

PERSIMMON BREAD

2/3 cup shortening
2 2/3 cups sugar
4 eggs
2 cups persimmon
  pulp
2/3 cup water
3 1/3 cups flour

2 teaspoons baking soda
1/2 teaspoon baking
  powder
1 teaspoon cinnamon
1 teaspoon cloves
2/3 cup nuts
2/3 cup raisins

Cream shortening and sugar until fluffy. Stir in eggs, pulp, and water. Blend in flour, baking soda, baking powder, and spices. Stir in nuts and raisins. Bake in loaf pans with waxed paper on the bottom. Bake at 350° for 70 minutes. *1 gallon of persimmons equals 4 cups of pulp. Makes 3 loaves - approximately 15 slices per loaf.

SKIERS' FRENCH TOAST

2 tablespoons corn syrup
1/2 cup butter or
  margarine
1 cup packed brown sugar
12 - 14 slices bread

5 eggs
1 1/2 cups milk
1 teaspoon vanilla
1/4 teaspoon salt
Cinnamon, to taste

Combine corn syrup, butter, and brown sugar, in saucepan and heat until mixture is syrup-like. Pour some into the bottom of 9" x 13" casserole dish. Layer bread into casserole, and pour remainder of syrup over bread. Beat together eggs, milk, vanilla, and salt. Pour over bread. Sprinkle cinnamon on top. Cover and refrigerate overnight. Bake at 350° for 45 minutes. *Serve with applesauce, and bacon or sausage. Makes 8 servings.

The Lookout Country Inn

14544 County Road 12 • Middlebury, IN 46540
219-825-9809
Innkeepers: Mary-Lou and Jim Wolfe

Come experience our comfortable hilltop home with its spectacular countryside view. **The Lookout** is situated on one of the highest spots in Elkhart County. In a quiet and restful setting, off the beaten path. Our 4 guest rooms, each with private bath, accommodate up to 12 persons. Overnight stays include a generous full breakfast served family-style in the sunroom on our 10' oak table. Enjoy the antique furnishings and our collections of oil lamps, teapots, and scales. For the pleasure of our guests, the common room features easy chairs, TV and VCR, books, magazines, games, and refrigerator to store any perishable purchases. After touring the area and shops, relax in our in-ground swimming pool or explore the walking trails through the wooded portion of our 8 acres. We are seasoned innkeepers and very knowledgeable about the area. We offer great hospitality, good food, and all the information you wish.

Rates: $$ Includes full breakfast. Children are welcome. No pets, please. Restricted smoking. We accept MasterCard and Visa.

APPLE BROWNIES

2/3 cup softened
  margarine
1 3/4 cups brown
  sugar
2 eggs
1 teaspoon vanilla
2 cups flour

2 teaspoons baking
  powder
1/4 teaspoon salt
1/3 cup chopped walnuts
1 cup raisins
1 cup chopped apple
Powdered sugar

Cream together margarine and brown sugar; add eggs and beat well. Add vanilla. Sift together flour, baking powder, and salt. Add to creamed mixture and beat well. Add walnuts, raisins, and apple; stir to blend. Spread in greased 9" x 13" pan. Bake at 350° for 30 to 35 minutes. Cool slightly, cut, remove from pan and roll in powdered sugar. *Great substitute for fruit breads. Makes 12 - 16 servings.

COUNTRY STYLE SAUSAGE GRAVY

1 - 1 1/2 pounds bulk
  breakfast sausage
1/2 green pepper, diced
1 medium onion, diced
4 ounce can sliced
  mushrooms

1/2 cup flour
4 cups milk (more or
  less)
Mrs. Dash No-Salt
  seasoning, or salt &
  pepper, to taste

Brown together sausage, green pepper, onion, and mushrooms, until vegetables are softened. Break up sausage while browning. Stir in flour and cook while stirring for one minute. Add milk, and cook to a medium thick gravy. Flavor with Mrs. Dash, or salt and pepper, to taste. Serve with baking powder biscuits. *Some persons have never experienced this great country treat, and it may be necessary to tell them to spoon the gravy over the biscuits. Makes 4 - 6 servings.

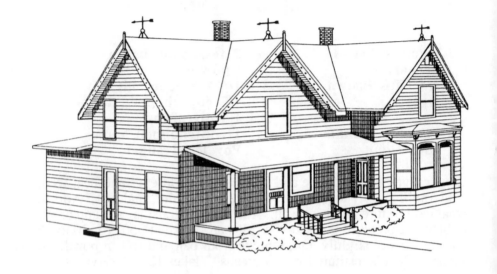

M & N Bed & Breakfast

215 North Detroit • LaGrange, IN 46761
219-463-2961   463-2699
Innkeepers: Sam and Estella Carney

This Victorian home was built in 1869. The upper level, first floor, and carriage house are devoted entirely to our guests. Enjoy the beautiful Victorian flower garden while sitting on the porch enjoying lemonade, iced tea, and homemade cookies. Wake up in the morning to fresh coffee or tea served in your room, and join us at your convenience for a full breakfast. We are proud to open the doors of this historic home to the public and provide for the comfort and enjoyment of our guests. All rooms have private baths, air conditioning, ceiling fans, and television.

Rates: $$ Includes full breakfast. Children are welcome. No pets, please. Restricted smoking. We accept MasterCard, Visa, and Discover.

CHEESE DANISH COFFEE CAKE

2 tubes Pillsbury crescent
   rolls
2 - 8 ounce pkgs. cream
   cheese, softened
3/4 cup sugar

1 egg, separated
1 teaspoon vanilla
1 teaspoon lemon juice
Powdered sugar and hot
   water for glaze

Spread one package of crescent rolls on bottom of 9" x 13" glass baking dish, pinch together to make crust. Cream together cream cheese, sugar, egg yolk, vanilla, and lemon juice. Spread on top of crust in pan. Cover with remaining package of crescent rolls. Beat egg white, spread on top crust. Bake at 350° for at least 30 to 40 minutes. Drizzle glaze over top after baking. Makes 12 - 16 servings.

HOT CIDER

1 gallon apple cider or
   apple juice
1 quart orange juice

Whole cloves, cinnamon,
   and nutmeg, to taste

Combine ingredients, and heat to simmer. Use spices as desired.

Market Street Guest House

253 East Market Street • Nappanee, IN 46550
219-773-2261   800-497-3791
Innkeeper: Sharon Bontrager

In 1922, Arthur Miller, the owner of the lumber and coal yard in
Nappanee purchased a lot and hired an architect from Chicago to
design a Georgian colonial brick house for his family. The house
features stained glass windows, open stairway, fireplace in living
room and a sun porch, now the breakfast room. The main bathroom
in the second floor hallway has the original tub and pedestal sink. In
1987 the house was purchased for a B&B. There are 5 guest rooms
with private baths. A full breakfast is served at the time the guest
chooses. Two blocks away are antique shops. Within 1 1/2 miles are
Amish Acres and Burkholder Dutch Village, an indoor mall with 400
plus booths of arts and crafts. Shipshewana and Notre Dame are just
45 minutes away. "Hospitality that remains in your memory long
after your visit," is our motto.

*Rates: $$ Includes full breakfast. Children are welcome. No pets or
smoking, please. We accept MasterCard, Visa, and Discover.*

Recipes From Market Street Guest House

CHICKEN SUPREME

2 cups cooked chicken
with broth
2 cups raw macaroni
2 cans cream of mush-
room soup or cream of
chicken soup
2 cups milk
Chopped onion, to taste

3 hard-boiled eggs
1/2 teaspoon salt
1/4 teaspoon pepper
3 tablespoons butter
1 cup Velveeta cheese,
cut into pieces or
Cheddar cheese,
shredded

Combine all ingredients in 9" x 13" casserole. Refrigerate at least 12 hours or overnight. Bake at 350° for one hour. Makes 6 - 8 servings.

FRUIT COCKTAIL PARFAIT

1 cup flour
1 cup white sugar
1 teaspoon baking soda
1/2 teaspoon salt
1 egg
2 cups fruit cocktail,
drained

2 - 3 tablespoons brown
sugar
1 cup Cool Whip
1/2 cup canned vanilla
pudding
Bananas and maraschino
cherries for garnish

Mix first four ingredients. Add egg and drained fruit. Place in 9" x 13" pan. Sprinkle brown sugar on top. Bake at 350° for 30 minutes. Cool. To serve, cut fruit cake into 1" squares. Spoon cake squares into bottom of parfait glass. Mix Cool Whip with pudding. Spoon Cool Whip mixture on top of cake squares in glass. Slice bananas onto Cool Whip mixture. Repeat layers to top of glass. Finish with a dab of Cool Whip and maraschino cherry. Makes 10 servings.

McCray Mansion Inn Bed & Breakfast

703 East Mitchell • Kendallville, IN 46755
219-347-3647
Innkeepers: Tim and Beth Kendrick & Ben and Tharon Shiley

A beautiful Georgian Colonial home in Kendallville, which has been made into a bed and breakfast. Home has three full floors plus a full basement, and is located on 5 city lots. The home has five bedrooms with four original baths. One has a 10-head shower. Two rooms have fireplaces. The home has a spectacular stairway of oak and walnut, which winds its way to the second floor and the basement. Has original crystal chandeliers, wall sconces, and floor coverings. The McCrays were the founders of the McCray Refrigerator and Cold Storage Company in 1890. The home has a large original McCray refrigerator which is in use today.

Rates: $$ Includes gourmet-style breakfast. Children are welcome. No pets, please. Restricted smoking. We accept MasterCard, Visa, and Am Ex.

Recipes From McCray Mansion Inn B & B

KIWI FRUIT DANISH

3 ounce pkg. refrigerator crescent dinner rolls
3 ounces cream cheese, softened
1 egg yolk
2 tablespoons sugar

1/2 teaspoon almond extract
1/2 cup apricot jam
2 - 3 kiwi fruits, pared & sliced

Unroll crescent dough and shape into triangles with equal sides. Combine cream cheese, egg yolk, sugar, and almond extract. Blend. Place 1 tablespoon cream cheese mixture in center of triangle, and top with kiwi fruit slice. Pull points of triangle together; pinch and seal. Bake at 375° for 12 to 15 minutes. Heat apricot jam. Put another kiwi fruit slice on top and glaze with jam. Makes 8 rolls or 4 servings.

MORNING GLORY MUFFINS

1 1/4 cups sugar
2 1/4 cups flour
1 tablespoon cinnamon
2 teaspoons baking soda
1/2 teaspoon salt
1/2 cup raisins
1/2 cup shredded coconut

2 cups grated carrots
1 apple, shredded
8 ounces crushed pineapple, drained
1/2 cup nuts
3 eggs
1 cup vegetable oil
1 teaspoon vanilla

Sift together sugar, flour, cinnamon, baking soda, and salt into large bowl. Add raisins, coconut, carrots, apple, pineapple, and nuts, and stir to combine. In separate bowl whisk eggs with oil, and vanilla. Pour this mixture into dry ingredients and blend well. Spoon batter into cupcake tins lined with muffin papers. Fill each to the brim. Bake at 350° for 35 minutes or until toothpick inserted in center comes out clean. Cool for 10 minutes before turning out. Muffins reach full flavor in 24 hours. Makes 16 large muffins.

Mulberry Inn & Gardens Bed & Breakfast

118 South Mulberry Street • Rising Sun, IN 47040
812-438-2206 800-235-3097
Owners: Jim and Janet Willis, Innkeeper: Betty Harris

We have five rooms for rent. All rooms include pillow top mattresses for that extra special touch. Our rooms feature queen size beds, with the exception of our "Jungle Room". It features a king size canopy bed, jacuzzi tub, and fireplace. All rooms have telephones, remote control color TV's, VCR's and private baths. We feature a full breakfast that will not allow you to go away hungry. We cater to our guests. You are pampered from the minute you arrive at our door. During the warmer months we have a large, peaceful, country garden to help you relax and reflect. Come try your luck on the Grand Victoria Riverboat, but go away remembering your stay!

Rates: $$$ - $$$$ Includes full breakfast. No children or pets, please. Restricted smoking. We accept MasterCard, Visa, Am Ex, and Discover.

Recipes From Mulberry Inn & Gardens B & B

BUTTERY CINNAMON SKILLET APPLES

4 medium cooking apples,
    peeled, cored &
    sliced in half
1/3 cup butter
1/2 - 3/4 cup sugar

1 tablespoon, plus 1
    teaspoon cornstarch
1 1/2 cups water
1/4 - 1/2 teaspoon
    cinnamon

Peel, core, and cut apples in half; set aside. Make sauce by melting butter in 10" skillet over medium heat; stir in sugar and cornstarch. Mix well and add remaining ingredients. Add apples to sauce, cover and cook over medium heat for 12 to 15 minutes, until apples are fork tender and sauce is thickened. Occasionally spoon sauce over apples as they cook. To serve, place 2 apple halves in dessert dish and ladle 1/2 cup sauce over each serving. Makes 4 servings.

HAM AND CHEESE STRATA

16 slices white bread,
    crusts removed
16 slices deli-style ham,
    thinly sliced
8 slices American cheese
8 slices Swiss cheese
3 cups milk
6 eggs, slightly beaten

1/2 teaspoon powdered
    mustard
1/2 teaspoon onion salt
2 cups Corn Flakes
    cereal, crushed
1/2 stick melted
    margarine

Layer in the following order in greased 9" x 13" x 2" casserole dish: 8 slices bread, 8 slices ham, 8 slices American cheese, 8 slices bread, 8 slices ham, 8 slices Swiss cheese. Mix milk, eggs, and seasonings; pour over layers. Combine crushed Corn Flakes and butter, sprinkle over top. Refrigerate overnight. Bake at 375° for 30 to 35 minutes or until puffed. Serve immediately. *Place cookie sheet in oven to catch spills. Makes 8 - 10 servings.

The Nuthatch Bed & Breakfast

7161 Edgewater Place • Indianapolis, IN 46240
317-257-2660
Innkeepers: Joan Hamilton Morris and Bernie Morris

The Nuthatch, in its quiet riverside setting, provides an ideal four season getaway. Built in the late Twenties, the house has a character all its own. From February's witch hazel to October's final roses, there is always something fragrant in the flower and herb gardens. Two guest rooms are reminiscent of Joan's childhood in Florida and upstate New York. The Adirondack Suite, filled with old wicker, rockers and Indian rugs from her Lake George home, offers a look at the river from its sitting room, solarium, and private terrace. The Wren's Nest is light-filled and open, with walls of soft peach (and tub of the same color), lavender and teal floral duvet, and modern rattan sitting area; imagine you are in the tropics, even with snow just outside. When the wrens nest in the redbud just outside, and the herb garden is in full perfume, the illusion becomes complete.

Rates: $$$ Includes full breakfast. Children over 12 are welcome, or both rooms may be rented. Limited availability for pets. Restricted smoking. We accept MasterCard, Visa, Am Ex, and Discover.

Recipes From The Nuthatch Bed & Breakfast

INDIANA CORNMEAL PANCAKES

1 3/4 cups stone ground cornmeal	2 large eggs (or EggBeaters)
1 1/2 teaspoons salt	2 1/4 cups buttermilk
3/4 teaspoon baking soda	1/3 cup canola or other
1/3 cup flour	light vegetable oil

Heat lightly oiled griddle or cast iron skillet. Stir together cornmeal, salt, baking soda, and flour. In separate bowl, mix eggs, buttermilk, and oil. When ready to cook, add buttermilk mixture to flour mixture. It should be the consistency of heavy cream with flecks of corn in it. If too thick, thin with a little more buttermilk. Pour batter by eighth cup amounts onto griddle to form slightly larger than silver dollar size pancakes. Cook until top has bubbles and bottom is golden (they may be more brown than regular pancakes). Turn and cook second side until it is also golden, about 1 minute. *Serve with boysenberry or raspberry syrup. Makes 4 generous servings.

INDIANA RASPBERRIES WITH ROSE CREAM

1 pint Indiana red and/or black raspberries	1 tablespoon confectioner's sugar
1/2 cup creme fraiche or sour cream	1/2 teaspoon rosewater
	Unsprayed rose petals

Toss berries together very gently in bowl. Whip together creme fraiche, confectioner's sugar, and rosewater. Spoon rose cream over berries and decorate with rose petals.

Oak Haven Bed & Breakfast

4975 North Hurricane Road (400 East) • Franklin, IN 46131
317-535-9491
Innkeepers: Alan and Brenda Smith

1913 home decorated with antiques and family treasures in all four guest rooms. (Private and shared bathrooms available). Oak woodwork and floors throughout our "haven". Nestled among stately trees that give a feeling of tranquility to our country setting. Play our 1914 player piano or relax on the porch swing. Perfect getaway for those with romance in their hearts or peaceful seclusion on their minds. A full country breakfast is served on fine china in the formal dining room. Located 1/2 mile from I-65 at the Whiteland exit; 25 minutes south of Indianapolis. Close to several golf courses including the "Legends of Indiana". Rustic Brown County is just 40 minutes away. Come experience our country hospitality at **Oak Haven Bed & Breakfast.**

Rates: $ - $$ Includes full breakfast. Children are welcome. No pets or smoking, please. We accept MasterCard and Visa.

Recipes From Oak Haven Bed & Breakfast

BETTY'S APPLE DUMPLINGS

2 cups sugar
2 cups water
1/4 teaspoon nutmeg
1 teaspoon cinnamon
1/8 teaspoon salt
1/4 cup butter or
  margarine
6 medium Rome apples
<u>Additional topping</u>:
6 teaspoons sugar

2 cups flour
3/4 cup butter flavor
  shortening
2 teaspoons baking
  powder
1/2 teaspoon salt
1/2 cup milk

6 teaspoons butter

Combine sugar, water, nutmeg, and cinnamon in saucepan. Cook 5 minutes over medium heat. Remove from heat and add salt and butter. Pare and core apples. Cut in shortening to flour; add baking powder and salt, then milk. Stir just until flour is moist. Divide into six equal parts and then roll into squares. Place one apple on each square; sprinkle with 1 teaspoon sugar and 1 teaspoon butter for topping on each. Fold corner of squares and pinch edges together to seal. Place in baking dish. Pour sauce over dumplings. Bake at 375° for 35 minutes until lightly brown. These freeze well after baking, and can be reheated and served. *Apples can be cut in half to make smaller dumplings. Makes 6 servings.

OAK HAVEN CINNAMON SYRUP

1 cup sugar
1/2 cup light corn syrup
1/4 cup water

2 tablespoons cinnamon
1/2 cup evaporated milk
1 1/2 tablespoons vanilla

In small saucepan, stir together sugar, corn syrup, water, and cinnamon, stirring constantly. Bring to boil over moderate heat. Boil for 2 minutes, then remove from heat. Stir in evaporated milk and vanilla. Cool at least 30 minutes. Syrup will thicken as it cools. May be stored in glass jar with lid and refrigerated for a couple of months. Serve warm over French toast or waffles. Makes 10 - 20 servings.

Oakwood Bed & Breakfast

9530 West U.S. Highway 136 • Jamestown, IN 46147
765-676-5114
Innkeepers: Bob and Marilyn Kernodle

Oakwood, built in 1990, was designed by the Kernodle's son when he was 15. The home features stunning oak trim and woodwork the owners made and hand-finished, and oak panel doors handcrafted by the Illinois Amish. Furnished in antiques, with a large china and glass collection . This reproduction of a stately Victorian home combines the charm and flavor of times gone by, with modern conveniences, including geothermal heating and cooling, and an exercise room (with billiard table) adjoining one guest room. Two rooms are available for guests. A common room contains a stocked refrigerator, TV and VCR with a library of movies as well as reading material and games. Whether you relax in the wicker furniture on the front porch, the enclosed back porch, or on the deck/gazebo, you can view Indiana countryside. Warm smiles, laughter, friendship, and a soothing relaxed atmosphere are yours at no extra cost.

Rates: $ - $$ Includes full breakfast. Children over age 12 are welcome. No pets or smoking, please.

Recipes From Oakwood Bed & Breakfast

APRICOT-ALMOND COFFEE CAKE

1 cup butter or margarine, softened
2 cups sugar
2 large eggs
1 teaspoon almond extract
2 cups all-purpose flour

1 teaspoon baking powder
1/4 teaspoon salt
8 ounces sour cream
1 cup sliced almonds
10 ounce jar apricot preserves

Beat butter at medium speed with electric mixer about 2 minutes or until creamy. Gradually add sugar; beat eggs in one at a time, beating mixture just until yellow disappears. Stir in almond extract. Combine flour, baking powder, and salt; add to butter mixture alternately with sour cream, beginning and ending with flour mixture. Mix at low speed just until blended after each addition. Place about one-third batter into greased and floured 12-cup bundt pan. Sprinkle with half of almonds, and dot with half of apricot preserves. Top with remaining batter; sprinkle with remaining almonds, and dot with remaining preserves. Bake at 350° for 50 to 55 minutes. Cool in pan on wire rack 10 to 15 minutes. *May substitute vanilla extract for almond extract, 1/2 cup chopped pecans for almonds, and 3 tablespoons brown sugar plus 2 teaspoons ground cinnamon for apricot preserves. Makes 1 - 10" cake.

HONEY FRUIT SALAD

1 large can pineapple chunks
2 medium oranges, peeled & sectioned
1 medium apple, peeled & diced

1 banana, peeled & sliced
1/2 cup chopped pecans (opt.)
1/2 cup orange juice
1 tablespoon lemon juice
1/4 cup honey

Combine first five ingredients in large bowl. Combine orange juice, lemon juice, and honey in small bowl; mix well. Pour over fruit, tossing gently. Chill thoroughly. *Coat the rim of sherbet dishes with lemon juice, dip in sugar until rim is frosted. Chill dishes until ready to add fruit salad. Garnish with fresh mint before serving.

Millikan

The Old Northside Bed & Breakfast

1340 North Alabama Street • Indianapolis, IN 46202
317-635-9123   FAX 317-635-9243   800-635-9127 (reservations)
Innkeepers: Susan Berry and Gary Hofmeister
www.hofmeister.com/b&b.htm

The Old Northside Bed & Breakfast, built in 1885, is situated in an historic, downtown neighborhood, convenient to I-65 and I-70. The inn features Romanesque Revival architecture, wrought iron fencing, an English garden, original maple wood floors, and hand-carved cherry and mahogany woodwork. Choose from five themed guest rooms with private baths, jacuzzi tubs, cable TV, and VCR's. The formal parlor, literary room, and bridal rooms boast fireplaces. Adorning the walls and ceilings are hand-painted murals, Lincrusta borders, and moiré fabric. A 1926 baby grand piano is featured in the music room. Candlelit, full breakfasts on depression glass, include gourmet fruit plates, freshly baked muffins, a hot entrée, and a variety of teas and coffee. A butler's pantry is stocked with complimentary beverages and snacks. Only a short walk downtown to historic neighborhoods, restaurants, theaters, museums, convention center, and numerous attractions. Only 15 minutes to Indy 500 Race Track, Indy Zoo, golf, tennis, swimming, & ice skating. Packages available.

Rates: $$$ - $$$$ Includes full breakfast. Children over age 12 are welcome. No pets or smoking, please. We accept MasterCard, Visa, Am Ex, and Discover.

Recipes From The Old Northside Bed & Breakfast

FLUFFY OMELET WITH CHEESE SAUCE

Omelet:
2 eggs, separated
(no substitutes)
3/4 cups cream
1 tablespoon seasoned
salt

Easy, Creamy Cheese
Sauce:
3/4 cup cubed Velveeta
cheese
1/4 cup cream

Separate egg whites from yolks. Add cream and seasoned salt to yolks. Beat egg white on high until stiff like meringue. Beat yolks on medium until blended well. Melt 1 teaspoon butter in each of two omelet pans. Gently blend egg yolks in with egg whites and pour half the mixture into each pan. Cook on medium-low heat until firm and lightly brown. Flip over and cook other side until brown. Fold in half on plate and pour cheese sauce over center of omelet. Garnish with fresh parsley. Makes 2 servings. For Cheese Sauce: Place Velveeta cheese and cream in saucepan and melt, stirring often. Do not let cheese at the bottom burn. You may have to add a little more cream for the smooth consistency you want.

GRIZZLE-KNUCKLES!

40 graham crackers,
finely crushed
2 cans sweetened
condensed milk

2 cups chocolate
chips
Powdered sugar

Crush graham crackers until fine. Mix crumbs in large bowl with sweetened condensed milk until moist. Add chocolate chips. Oil bottom of 9" x 11" pan. Pour mixture into pan and spread evenly. Bake at 350° until firm in center. Remove from oven; let cool slightly. Cut into squares. Place powdered sugar into Ziploc bag and place squares in bag. Shake until fully coated with sugar. Remove and arrange on platter. Warning: Do not inhale while biting into these delicious bars!

Olde Buffalo Inn Bed & Breakfast

1061 Parkwood Drive • Nappanee, IN 46550
219-773-2223   773-4275 FAX   888-773-2223
Innkeepers: Ann and Larry Lakins

The history of **the Inn** extends over 150 years. Originally built in 1840 by a pioneer farmer, the house precedes Nappanee by 34 years. By the turn of the century it had acquired the name the Buffalo Farm, during a time when the bison were characteristic of the area. The barn echoes with a history of its own as many of the Amish held church there. Today the original farmhouse still exists - with restorations and additional rooms constructed - thus, modern conveniences. Original basement was transformed into a replica of a tavern found in Williamsburg, Virginia. The property is picturesque with the huge red barn, traditional windmill, carriage house, with white picket fence on 2 1/2 acres, with six guest rooms with private bath (4 in the old part and 2 in the addition).

Rates: $$ - $$$ Includes full breakfast. Children over age 10 are welcome. No pets, please. Restricted smoking. We accept MasterCard, Visa, and Discover.

Recipes From Olde Buffalo Inn Bed & Breakfast

CHRISTMAS FUDGE (SMOOTH)

9 3/4 ounce plain milk chocolate bar
12 ounces chocolate bits
2 semi-sweet baking chocolate squares, cut finely
2 cups broken pecans

1 pint marshmallow creme
1 tablespoon vanilla
1 large can evaporated milk
4 1/2 cups sugar
1/4 pound butter
1/4 pound oleo

In large bowl place chocolate bar, chocolate bits, chocolate squares, pecans, marshmallow creme, vanilla, and set aside. In heavy pan, put milk, sugar, butter, and oleo; bring to a boil and let boil 6 minutes. Pour over mixture in the large bowl and stir until all is melted. Pour into buttered pan to set. Cut when cold. Store in refrigerator. Makes 4 pounds of fudge.

PECAN PIE

1 cup white corn syrup
1 cup dark brown sugar
1/3 teaspoon salt
1/3 cup melted butter

3 large eggs
1 teaspoon vanilla
1 - 9" unbaked pie shell
1 cup whole large pecans

Mix corn syrup, brown sugar, salt, and melted butter. Add slightly beaten eggs, and vanilla. Pour into unbaked pie shell. Sprinkle pecans into filling. Bake at 350° for about 45 minutes. Makes 6 - 8 servings.

The Oliver Inn Bed & Breakfast

630 West Washington Street • South Bend, IN 46601
219-232-4545   219-288-9788 FAX
oliver@michiana.org
http://michiana.org/users/oliver
Innkeepers: Richard and Venera Monahan

The Oliver Inn Bed & Breakfast offers a "Turn of the Century" feeling with today's most important amenities. Nine beautifully furnished rooms, private baths, phone, central air, and TV. Several feature a fireplace, private balcony or double jacuzzi. Located in the historic downtown district of South Bend, 90 minutes from Chicago, and only 2 miles from the Indiana Toll Road Exit #77. Located next door to the famous Tippecanoe Place Restaurant (Studebaker Mansion). The largest B&B in South Bend, on a one acre estate with carriage house. Common areas include a cozy library with fireplace, and baby grand piano with computer disk system, front parlor, dining room with fireplace and Waterford crystal chandelier, and a Butler's Pantry with complimentary beverages and snacks. Several porches are provided for relaxing outdoors. Wicker furniture, plantation rockers, and lawn swings provide lounging areas. Badminton, bocce balls, and lawn croquet are provided for our guests.

Rates: $$ - $$$$ Includes continental plus breakfast. Children are welcome. Limited availability for pets. No smoking, please. We accept MasterCard, Visa, Am Ex, and Discover.

Recipes From The Oliver Inn Bed & Breakfast

BACON ROLL-UPS

1 pound bacon	1/4 cup mayonnaise
1 can whole water	1/4 cup chili sauce
chestnuts	1/2 cup brown sugar

Cut each bacon strip into thirds, wrap a water chestnut, and secure with toothpick. Mix mayonnaise, chili sauce, and brown sugar together, and pour over bacon roll-ups. Bake at 350° for 45 minutes. Makes 6 servings.

BEEF & PICKLE ROLL-UPS

8 ounces cream cheese, softened	2 tablespoons Worcestershire sauce
2 tablespoons dried onion soup mix	5 ounce jar dried beef
Few drops of Tabasco sauce, to taste	24 ounce jar pickle spears, cut lengthwise into thirds

Mix first four ingredients together. Spread dried beef slices with cream cheese mixture. Place pickle on edge of dried beef slice and roll up. Serve whole or cut into slices and serve on crackers. Makes 8 servings.

Recipes From The Oliver Inn Bed & Breakfast

CLAIRE'S CRAZY CAKE

1 1/2 cups flour
1 cup sugar
3 rounded tablespoons cocoa
1 teaspoon salt

1 teaspoon baking soda
6 tablespoons oil
1 tablespoon vinegar
1 teaspoon vanilla
1 cup water

Sift flour, sugar, cocoa, salt, and baking soda into oblong pan. Stir well with fork. Mix oil, vinegar, and vanilla in a cup. Make 3 holes in dry mixture and pour liquid mixture into holes. Pour water over all and stir well with fork. Bake at 350° for 25 minutes. Makes 6 servings. *In Memory of my Mother, Clarice E. Golino - she loved to whip up this cake on a minute's notice.

EGG & BREAD BREAKFAST

12 slices bread, diced or torn into small pieces
1 1/4 pounds shredded Colby and/or Swiss cheese
2 cups milk

6 eggs
Salt, pepper, & paprika, to taste
1 cup diced ham and/or green onions (opt.)
1 stick butter

Mix bread and shredded cheese together in casserole dish sprayed with cooking spray. Mix together milk, eggs, seasonings, ham, and green onions (if desired). Pour over bread mixture. Refrigerate overnight. Melt butter and pour over mixture. Bake at 350° for 45 minutes.

Recipes From The Oliver Inn Bed & Breakfast

MONKEY BREAD

2 tubes Pillsbury Grands
  biscuits
1 cup sugar
1/4 cup cinnamon

1 stick butter
1 cup brown sugar
1/2 cup chopped
  nuts

Cut each biscuit into fourths. Mix sugar and cinnamon together in bag, and shake biscuits until coated. Save sugar-cinnamon mixture for future use. Arrange biscuits in bundt pan sprayed with cooking spray. Melt butter and mix in brown sugar. Bring to a boil and lower heat, cooking approximately 2 minutes. Mix in nuts. Pour over biscuits, lifting edges, allowing mixture to reach bottom of pan. Bake at 350° for 30 minutes. Makes 8 servings.

POP POP GOLINO'S REAL ITALIAN TOMATO SAUCE

1/4 cup cooking oil
4 - 6 cloves chopped
  garlic
1/2 pound ground beef
1/2 pound ground Italian
  sausage (regular or hot)
2 - 28 ounce cans whole
  tomatoes, chopped &
  undrained

2 - 12 ounce cans tomato
  paste
3 - 8 ounce cans tomato
  sauce
1 tablespoon oregano
3 tablespoons sugar
1/2 cup water
Salt, pepper, & crushed
  red pepper, to taste

Brown garlic, ground beef, and sausage in oil. Then add remainder of ingredients. Bring to a boil, then lower heat. Simmer 2 to 3 hours, stirring often. *Can be frozen for future meals.

Orchard Hill Inn & Cabin

1958 North State Road 135 • Nashville, IN 47448
800-968-7266
Innkeeper & Storyteller: Pete Sebert

Ten room inn, large community room and deck overlooking two acres wooded grounds and fishing pond, herb, and flower gardens. Affordable comfort and country charm, just 1 1/2 miles from Nashville. Early American furnishings, rocking chairs, antiques, quilts, and country hospitality served daily with fresh baked fruit muffins and a continental breakfast. Each room with rustic open beam ceilings and knotty pine paneling, tastefully decorated with wall-to-wall carpeting, air-conditioning, cable TV. Six rooms with 2 double beds, 4 queen or king poster or canopy, reminding the guest of a quieter time where people still sit on the porch munching our muffins, or feel the ripple of a friendly smile. Cabin sleeps 8, fireplace in spacious living room, kitchen, sun room, antique bedrooms. Porch overlooking fishing pond and grove of pine trees.

Rates: $ - $$$$ Includes continental breakfast. Children are welcome. Limited availability for pets. No smoking, please. We accept MasterCard, Visa, Am Ex, and Discover.

Recipes From Orchard Hill Inn & Cabin

APPLE OR FRUIT MUFFINS

1 cup sliced apples or
  other seasonal fresh
  fruit, mixed with sugar
  & dash of cinnamon,
  to taste
1/3 cup butter
1/3 cup brown sugar

2 eggs, beaten
1 cup milk
2 cups flour
4 teaspoons baking
  powder
Dash of salt

Mix fruit with sugar/cinnamon mixture. Cream butter and brown sugar. Add beaten eggs, milk, and dry ingredients. Stir in fruit. Do not overmix. Fill greased muffin cups 1/2 full. Bake at 375° for 20 to 25 minutes. Makes 12 large or 16 small muffins.

STRAWBERRY SHORTCAKE MUFFINS

2 1/3 cups Bisquick
  Original baking mix
3 tablespoons sugar
1/2 cup milk

3 tablespoons melted
  butter
1 quart strawberries,
  hulled and washed

Stir baking mix, sugar, milk, and melted butter together. Chop 1/2 quart of strawberries almost to juice. Mix into baking mix batter. Slice remaining 1/2 quart of strawberries, sweeten to taste, and stir throughout batter. Bake at 425° for 10 to 12 minutes. Garnish with fresh strawberry slices if desired. Makes 12 muffins.

The Prairie House Bed & Breakfast

495 East 900 North • Leesburg, IN 46538
219-658-9211
Innkeepers: Everett and Marie Tom

The Prairie House Bed & Breakfast is located on a working farm located midway between Leesburg and Milford, one mile east of State Road 15 on 900 North. We have four guest rooms, each individually decorated, with queen size beds, down comforters, air conditioning, and cable TV. Farm tours can be arranged to watch planting, harvesting, detasseling seed corn, or view Everett's cow/calf operation. Located side of Amish country, we are near many lakes with fishing, swimming, skiing, and boating available. Grace College, Amish Acres, Wagon Wheel Playhouse, Shipshewana Flea Market, Notre Dame, the Old Bag Factory in Goshen and many antique stores are within easy driving distance. Many excellent restaurants are also in the area. So, come join us for a getaway -- good food, and relaxing atmosphere, or plan an overnight retreat and make use of our meeting room, and "Prepare to be Pampered".

Rates: $$ Includes full breakfast. Children are welcome. No pets or smoking, please. We accept MasterCard and Visa.

Recipes From The Prairie House Bed & Breakfast

ENGLISH SCONES WITH CLOTTED CREAM

2 cups all-purpose flour
1/2 cup sugar
2 teaspoons baking
 powder
1/4 cup cold butter
1 cup raisins

1/2 cup milk
1 egg
1/2 cup heavy cream
2 tablespoons powdered
 sugar
1/2 cup sour cream

In bowl combine flour, sugar, and baking powder. Cut in butter until mixture resembles fine crumbs. Stir in raisins. Beat milk, and egg; add to dry ingredients, stirring lightly. Turn onto lightly floured board; roll to 1" thickness. Cut with 2 1/2" biscuit cutter. Place on ungreased baking sheet. Bake at 425° for 10 to 15 minutes or until golden brown. Makes 10 scones. *Blueberries can be substituted for raisins. For Clotted Cream: In chilled bowl, beat heavy cream until medium stiff peaks form. Add powdered sugar during last part of beating. Fold in sour cream. Refrigerate. Use instead of butter or margarine.

SAUSAGE SWIRLS

4 cups all-purpose flour
1/4 cup cornmeal
2 tablespoons sugar
2 teaspoons baking
 powder

1 teaspoon salt
2/3 cup vegetable oil
3/4 - 1 cup milk
2 pounds uncooked
 bulk pork sausage

In large bowl, combine flour, cornmeal, sugar, baking powder, and salt. Stir in oil until mixture resembles coarse crumbs. Gradually stir in enough milk to form a soft dough. Turn onto floured board; knead lightly for 30 seconds. Roll into 2 - 16" x 10" rectangles. Crumble uncooked sausage over dough to within 1/2" on all sides. Carefully roll up from 16" end. Wrap in foil; chill for at least one hour. Cut into 1/2" slices; place 1" apart on ungreased baking sheets. Bake at 400° for 15 to 20 minutes or until lightly browned. Serve warm or cold. Store in refrigerator. Makes about 4 dozen swirls.

Prairie Manor Bed & Breakfast

66398 U.S. 33 South • Goshen, IN 46526
800-791-3952
Innkeepers: Jean and Hesston Lauver

Come enjoy the country and our English country manor style home. Situated on twelve acres of grass, shade trees, flowers, meadowland, and woods. **Prairie Manor** was built in the 1920's by a New York City Wall Street banker. The living room replicates the builder's favorite painting at the Metropolitan Museum of Art -- an English baronial hall featuring a fireplace big enough to walk into. Relax in the wood-paneled library with window seats and a fireplace. The house has many interesting architectural details such as arched doorways, wainscoting, and a hidden compartment. **Prairie Manor** offers three bedrooms and one suite, all with private baths. Televisions, telephone, FAX, swimming pool, and a horse barn are available. We are located in the center of Amish country. A full breakfast that takes advantage of local seasonal produce is served.

Rates: $$ - $$$ Includes full breakfast. Children are welcome. No pets or smoking, please. We accept MasterCard and Visa.

Recipes From Prairie Manor Bed & Breakfast

FRESH VEGETABLE FRITTATA

1 large sweet red or green pepper, chopped
1 cup sliced fresh mushrooms
1 1/2 cups shredded Cheddar cheese, divided
1/4 pound asparagus, cut into 1" pieces (pre-cooked)

7 large eggs, lightly beaten
1/2 cup mayonnaise
1/2 teaspoon salt
2 tablespoons chopped fresh basil or 2 teaspoons dried basil
1 tomato, sliced

Layer pepper, mushrooms, and half of cheese in lightly greased 9 1/2" deep-dish pie plate. Top with asparagus and remaining cheese. Combine eggs and remaining ingredients, except tomato. Pour evenly over cheese. Top with tomato slices. Bake at 375° for 35 minutes or until knife inserted in center comes out clean. Let stand 5 minutes. Serve hot or at room temperature. Makes 4 servings.

PEACHES AND CREAM CHEESE CAKE

3/4 cup flour
1 teaspoon baking powder
3 1/4 ounce box dry vanilla pudding mix (not instant)
3 tablespoons margarine, softened
1 egg
1/2 cup milk

15 - 20 ounce can sliced peaches, drained
3 tablespoons reserved peach juice
8 ounces cream cheese, softened
1/2 cup sugar
1 tablespoon sugar
1/2 teaspoon cinnamon

Drain peaches, reserve 3 tablespoons juice. Mix first six ingredients in bowl. Beat 2 minutes with mixer at medium speed. Pour into greased 9" - 10" pie pan. Place drained fruit over batter. Mix reserved peach juice, cream cheese, & 1/2 cup sugar. Beat 2 minutes at medium speed. Spoon over batter to within 1" of edge. Combine 1 tablespoon sugar and cinnamon. Sprinkle over top. Bake at 350° for 30 to 35 minutes. Store in refrigerator. Makes 4 - 6 servings.

Royer's 1836 Log House Bed & Breakfast

22781 County Road 38 • Goshen, IN 46526
219-533-1821
Innkeepers: Raymond and Barbara Royer

Most often our guests refer to their stay here as being serene and very quieting. Our log house has large family size rooms with antique claw foot tubs in each private bath. The little romantic honeymoon cottage is rustic and has a small fireplace. All six guest rooms have either king or queen size beds. We have lots of porches with swings to enjoy the beautiful outdoors, and a library of good books. Our full family-style breakfast is an excellent beginning for those who want to spend the day shopping or sightseeing. And our own gift shop in the loft has a variety of unique items.

Rates: $$ - $$$ Includes full breakfast. Children are welcome. No pets or smoking, please. We accept MasterCard, Visa, and Discover.

Recipes From Royer's 1836 Log House B & B

CORNMEAL ROLLS

1/3 cup cornmeal	1 tablespoon yeast
1/2 cup sugar	1/2 cup warm water
2 teaspoons salt	2 beaten eggs
1/2 cup oleo	4 - 6 cups flour
2 cups milk	

Cook first five ingredients together until thick - cool to lukewarm. Dissolve yeast in warm water. Add to cornmeal. Stir in eggs and flour. Let rise in refrigerator overnight. Roll out and cut with 2 1/2" round cutter. Let rise at least one hour. Brush with melted butter and sprinkle with cornmeal. Bake at 350° until lightly browned. *Delicious to use for egg muffins. Makes 3 dozen rolls.

LAZY DAY DUFF

1/2 cup butter	1 tablespoon baking
1 cup flour	powder
1/2 cup sugar	2/3 cup milk
1/8 teaspoon salt	2 cups sweetened fruit

Melt butter in 8" baking dish. Mix together flour, sugar, salt, and baking powder. Add milk. Pour into butter in baking dish. Pour fruit over batter. Bake at 375° for 35 minutes. Makes 6 - 8 servings.

Schussler House Bed & Breakfast

514 Jefferson Street • Madison, IN 47250
812-273-2068
Innkeepers: Judy and Bill Gilbert

Experience the quiet elegance of a circa 1849 Federal/Greek Revival home, tastefully combined with today's modern conveniences. **Schussler House** is located in the heart of Madison's Historic District, a pleasant walk from antique shops, historic sites, restaurants, and the beautiful Ohio River Walk. This beautifully renovated home offers three spacious guest rooms decorated with antiques and reproductions. Specially selected wallcoverings and fabrics, lace curtains, and inviting reading areas make each room unique. A sumptuous, tastefully prepared breakfast is served on china and crystal in the formal dining room. Air-conditioned for your summer comfort, and winter days are enhanced by fires in the parlor and dining room. Enjoy the finest in accommodations at **Schussler House Bed & Breakfast.**

Rates: $$$ Includes full breakfast. Children over age 12 are welcome. No pets or smoking, please. We accept MasterCard, Visa, and Discover.

APPLE STRATA FRENCH TOAST

1 loaf Italian bread,
crust removed, cubed
2 tablespoons butter
4 cups peeled, sliced
tart apples
2 teaspoons cinnamon,
divided

1/2 cup brown sugar,
divided
4 eggs, beaten
2 cups milk
1 teaspoon vanilla

Trim bread, cube, and set aside. Sauté sliced apples in skillet with butter, and 1/4 cup brown sugar until tender. Spread on bottom of greased 9" x 13" baking dish. Spread bread cubes over apple slices. Sprinkle top with 1 teaspoon cinnamon and 1/4 cup brown sugar. In bowl, whisk beaten eggs, milk, 1 teaspoon cinnamon, and vanilla. Pour over bread cubes. Refrigerate overnight. In the morning, preheat oven to 350° and bake for 45 minutes or until lightly browned and beginning to puff. Cut into squares and serve with Apple Cinnamon Syrup - recipe below. Makes 8 servings.

APPLE CINNAMON SYRUP

1/2 cup sugar
3 teaspoons cornstarch
3/4 teaspoon cinnamon

1 cup apple juice or cider
1 tablespoon lemon juice
2 tablespoons butter

In small saucepan, combine sugar, cornstarch, and cinnamon. Add apple juice, and lemon juice. Over medium heat, cook and stir until mixture starts to bubble. Continue stirring and cooking for an additional 2 minutes. Remove from heat and add butter. Serve warm over Apple Strata French Toast - recipe above. Makes 1 1/3 cups.

Spring View Bed & Breakfast

63189 County Road 31 • Goshen, IN 46526
219-642-3997
Innkeepers: Phil and Roz Slabaugh

Spring View Bed & Breakfast is a new home located on a small private lake on 48 acres in the heart of Amish country. You can relax as you stroll our waterfront, or rest in the screened lakeside sitting room, or enjoy bird watching or reading in the other sitting room. Enjoy a luxurious steam bath or whirlpool tub in the privacy of your own room. There are five rooms with private baths, a two bedroom suite available, and a special honeymoon room with a double steam whirlpool tub. Full breakfast is served in the sunroom. Paddleboats, fishing equipment, and bicycles are available for your pleasure. A campfire area is available. Meeting room and central air. Near Notre Dame University, (1 hour) Goshen College, (3 miles) Shipshewana Flea Market, city and county parks, and area golf courses, with snowmobiling trail on our property. Located 3 hours from Indianapolis and Chicago.

Rates: $$ Includes full breakfast. Children are welcome. No pets or smoking, please. We accept MasterCard, Visa, Am Ex, and Discover.

Recipes From Spring View Bed & Breakfast

ALMOND PEACH MUFFINS

1 1/2 cups all-purpose flour
1 cup sugar
3/4 teaspoon salt
1/2 teaspoon baking soda
2 eggs
1/2 cup vegetable oil
1/2 teaspoon vanilla extract

1/8 teaspoon almond extract
1 1/4 cups chopped, peeled, fresh peaches (or 16 ounce can peaches, drained & chopped)
1/2 cup chopped almonds

In large bowl combine flour, sugar, salt, and baking soda. In another bowl, beat eggs, oil, and extracts; stir into dry ingredients just until moistened. Fold in peaches and almonds. Fill greased or paper-lined muffin cups 3/4 full. Bake at 375° for 20 to 25 minutes or until muffins test done. Cool in pan for 10 minutes before removing to wire rack. Makes 12 muffins.

OATMEAL PEANUT COOKIES

1 cup shortening (not butter)
1 cup white sugar
1 cup brown sugar
2 eggs
1 1/2 cups all-purpose flour

3 cups quick oatmeal
1 teaspoon baking soda
1/2 pound salted peanuts
2 teaspoons vanilla extract

Cream shortening and sugars. Add eggs. In separate bowl combine flour, oatmeal, baking soda, and peanuts. Add vanilla to shortening mixture. Stir in dry ingredients. Shape into balls. A small ice cream scoop works well. Bake at 375° for 10 to 12 minutes. Do not overbake. *I won a blue ribbon at the County Fair with this recipe. Makes 3 dozen cookies.

Stone Soup Inn

1304 North Central Avenue • Indianapolis, IN 46202
317-639-9550
Innkeepers: Jeneane Life and Jordan Rifkin

Built in 1901, and located in the heart of the historic Old Northside, **Stone Soup Inn** offers all the beauty and comfort of a turn-of-the-century home. Decorated with Mission-style and Victorian-era antiques, guests will find a comfortable, convenient place to stay as they explore nearby historic sites, Indianapolis' theater district, and downtown attractions. The Victorian Room contains a beautiful tiled fireplace, and is accented with exquisite architectural detail and beautiful floral bouquets. The Craftsman Room is furnished with Mission-style antiques, and shares a bath with Victorian Room. Lily's Room holds queen wicker bed, oriental desk and trunk, and bay window seat. Private bath featuring 2-person jacuzzi tub. The Blue Room is filled with antique furniture, tiled fireplace and private bath with steam shower. All rooms have VCR and cable TV. Complimentary snacks and hot/cold beverages. FAX machine available. Innkeeper speaks both German and Japanese languages.

Rates: $$$ Includes full or continental breakfast. Children over age 12 are welcome. No pets or smoking, please. We accept MasterCard, Visa, Am Ex, and Discover.

Recipes From Stone Soup Inn

GRANDMA MARY'S CHEESE STRATA

8 slices bread, crusts
trimmed
Soft butter for bread
2 1/2 cups shredded
sharp Cheddar cheese

4 eggs, slightly beaten
2 1/2 cups milk
1 teaspoon salt
4 teaspoons dry
mustard

Stack 4 slices of bread (2 stacks); trim and butter each slice. Alternate layers of bread and cheese in 9" x 13" baking dish, ending with cheese. Mix other ingredients, pour over layers. Chill overnight or longer. Bake at 350° for at least one hour, perhaps longer, depending on oven. Make sure center tests done. Makes 4 - 8 servings.

STONE SOUP (Stone optional!)

Bouquet Garni:
1 stalk chopped celery,
with leaves
6 whole peppercorns
1 bay leaf
Tarragon and basil,
to taste
Soup Base:
10 cups chicken broth
1 medium onion,
quartered
1 1/2 cups diced celery
1 1/2 cups sliced &
peeled carrots

2 medium potatoes, cut
into bite-sized pieces
1 package frozen mixed
vegetables
1 1/2 cups cooked
rigatoni pasta
1/3 cup barley
Salt & pepper, to taste
Garlic powder & sage,
to taste
Onion Roux:
1 small onion, diced
Flour & margarine,
as needed

For Bouquet Garni: Place ingredients in 6" piece of cheesecloth and tie ends. Add to chicken broth, and combine with medium onion, celery, and carrots in large stock pot and cook for 45 minutes on medium heat. Add potato, mixed vegetables, cooked rigatoni, barley, and onion roux (Add roux slowly). For Onion Roux: Sauté small onion until golden brown. Add flour and margarine to make roux. Cook until potatoes are soft; add salt, pepper, garlic powder, and sage to taste. Remove Bouquet Garni and serve with crusty bread. Makes 10 servings.

Story Inn

6404 South State Road 135 • Nashville, IN 47448
812-988-2273
Innkeepers: Bob and Gretchen Haddix

Our main building is an 1850's General Store that houses our award-winning restaurant. We can accommodate up to 70 people. We also feature, during warm weather, a screened back porch with a garden-patio view for dining. We have guest accommodations for up to 38 persons which include 2 doubles, 6 suites, and 4 cottages. Some cottages offer either full or partial kitchens. Four of the rooms are upstairs in the main building, with the rest being in cottage units on the village grounds. Our quaintly decorated rooms (some in 100-year-old country houses) feature no telephones, televisions, or radios. Throw out your clock, if you wish, and step back in time. The price of your room includes all applicable taxes and breakfast for each guest. Evening gourmet meals are available by advance reservations.

Rates: $$$ - $$$$ Includes full breakfast. Children are welcome. Limited availability for pets. No smoking, please. We accept MasterCard, Visa, and Discover.

Recipes From Story Inn

CHOCOLATE FUDGE PEANUT BUTTER PIE

3/4 cup smooth peanut butter
2 cups powdered sugar
1/2 tablespoon real butter, softened
1 deep dish pie shell (9" - 10"), pre-baked

3 ounces real butter, softened
1 cup brown sugar
2 teaspoons vanilla
3 eggs
1/4 cup flour
12 ounces melted bittersweet chocolate

Mix peanut butter, powdered sugar, and 1/2 tablespoon butter slowly until thick. Roll into walnut size balls and refrigerate. Mix 3 ounces butter, brown sugar, vanilla, and eggs with mixer. Add flour and melted chocolate; mix until smooth. Have baked pie shell ready. Place refrigerated peanut butter balls in shell and pour fudge mixture over top. Bake at 350° for 30 to 40 minutes until top looks dry. When completely cool, cut into approximately 8 - 10 wedges. Dangerously rich - cut small pieces!!!

MAPLE PECAN PIE

4 large eggs
1 cup granulated sugar
1/2 teaspoon salt
1 cup light corn syrup
1/2 cup real maple syrup

1/2 cup real butter, melted & cooled (not margarine
1 1/2 cups pecans
1 - 9" fluted pie shell, unbaked

Preheat oven to 400°. Using a wire whip, whisk all ingredients except pecans until well-blended. Place pecans in bottom of prepared pie shell and pour liquid mixture over top. Gently stir up pecans to surface. (You can arrange pecan halves in concentric circles at this time or just leave them jumbled.) Place pie in oven for 15 minutes. Reduce heat to 325° and bake for 40 to 50 minutes until puffed with a dry appearance. Let cool for one hour. It will sink and flatten out smooth. *It also refrigerates well. Makes 8 servings.

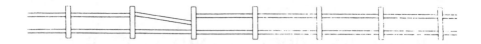

A BED AND BREAKFAST

SULINA FARM
SETTLED 1804

Sulina Farm Bed & Breakfast

10052 U. S. Highway 52 • Brookville, IN 47012
800-486-8079
Innkeeper: Mr. Tristan G. Ariens

The Sulina Farm Bed & Breakfast is an endearing turn-of-the-century farm house elegantly renovated to offer the best in Bed & Breakfast accommodations in Southeast Indiana. Set on the outskirts of the lovely town of Brookville, **Sulina Farm B&B** has three bedrooms with private baths, cozy sitting rooms, and comfortable porches. Come and stay with us so you can take a walk to the Whitewater River, and feel at home in a relaxed atmosphere of Hoosier hospitality!

Rates: $$ Includes full breakfast. Children are welcome. No pets, please. Restricted smoking. We accept MasterCard, Visa, Am Ex, and Discover.

Recipes From Sulina Farm Bed & Breakfast

AVOCADO SALAD

3 avocados
1 cup pineapple chunks
1 cup grapes, halved
2 oranges (peeled &
cut into pieces)

French dressing for
marinade
Lettuce leaves
Fresh mint for garnish

Cut avocados into halves lengthwise and scoop out pulp with a French vegetable cutter. Save shells. Combine avocado pulp with other fruit and marinate in French dressing for about 20 minutes. Fill avocado shells with fruit mix and serve on lettuce leaves. Garnish with fresh mint. Makes 6 servings.

SOUR CREAM POTATOES

4 cups sliced, cooked
potatoes
1/4 cup chopped onion
2 tablespoons butter
1 cup sour cream
2 tablespoons water

2 eggs, well-beaten
1 teaspoon salt
Dash of pepper
1 cup shredded sharp
Cheddar cheese

Cook potatoes in salted water until done. Sauté onions in butter. Combine with sour cream, water, eggs, salt, and pepper. Place drained potatoes in 1-quart buttered casserole dish. Pour sour cream sauce over them. Top with shredded cheese and bake at 350° for 20 to 25 minutes. Makes 6 servings.

Thorpe House Country Inn

P.O. Box 36, 19049 Clayborne Street • Metamora, IN 47030
765-647-5425
Innkeepers: Mike and Jean Owens

Circa 1840's, this peaceful, easy feeling **Inn** is a typical middle-class Victorian clapboard home with a "gingerbready" front porch. Only one block from the restored Whitewater Canal, listed on the National Register of Historic Sites. Four cozy guest rooms and a 2-room suite are furnished with antiques/country accessories/private baths. No in-room phone, TV, radio, or alarm clock to disturb your escape from routine. Enjoy a hearty breakfast before exploring 100+ shoppes/museums in this quaint historic village. Transportation options include excursion train, horsedrawn carriage, or canalboat. Although "we are over 150 years away", we're conveniently located between Indianapolis and Cincinnati. Recreational diversions - canoeing, hiking, bicycling, fishing, water sports, golf, exploring Indian Mounds - are all nearby. Family-style dining room is open to the public. Seasonal.

Rates: $$ - $$$$ Includes full breakfast. Children are welcome.
Pets are allowed. Smoking is permitted. We accept MasterCard,
Visa, Am Ex, and Discover.

Recipes From Thorpe House Country Inn

CREAM CHEESE MUFFINS

1 egg
3/4 cup milk
1/2 cup vegetable oil
2 cups flour
1/3 cup sugar

3 teaspoons baking
   powder
1/2 teaspoon salt
Powdered sugar

Filling:
4 ounces cream cheese,
   softened
1/4 cup sugar
1 egg

1/2 teaspoon grated
   lemon peel
1/8 teaspoon vanilla

Mix Filling ingredients together with mixer. Set aside. Heat oven to 350°. Oil or spray bottoms only of medium muffin tins. Beat egg, stir in milk, and oil; set aside. Mix flour, sugar, baking powder, and salt until well blended. Pour liquids all at once into flour; stir until moistened. Fill cups about half full; spoon one teaspoon filling onto batter. Top with batter to fill 3/4 full. Bake for 30 to 35 minutes. Don't brown; should be light in color. Roll hot muffins in powdered sugar. Makes about 8 muffins.

"TO THE RESCUE" SOUR CREAM COFFEE CAKE

1 box yellow or white
   cake mix
3/4 cup vegetable oil
4 eggs
1/2 cup sugar

8 ounces sour cream
3 tablespoons brown
   sugar
1 tablespoon cinnamon

Mix cake mix, oil, eggs, sugar, and sour cream; beat together well. In separate bowl, mix brown sugar and cinnamon. Pour half of batter into greased and floured bundt pan. Add brown sugar-cinnamon mixture to remaining batter and pour over the top. Bake at 350° for 50 to 60 minutes. Makes 12 servings.

Varns Guest House

P.O. Box 125, 205 South Main Street • Middlebury, IN 46540
219-825-9666   800-398-5424
Innkeepers: Carl and Diane Eash

Elegance and superb taste adorn this beautiful Colonial Revival home built in 1898. The historical value adds to the ambience of the home that was built by Ellsworth Varns, great-grandfather of the current owner. Located in Amish country on Middlebury's beautiful tree-lined Main Street; guests relax on the wraparound porch as Amish buggies clip-clop past the Inn. The five guest rooms each have a private bath with one room featuring a whirlpool tub. Breakfast with Geraldine is a special treat which features her homemade pastries. Recently featured in <u>Midwest Living</u> magazine, the **Varns Guest House** is inspected and approved annually by trained professionals from IBBA, ABBA, and AAA. Visit the many fine shops and restaurants nearby as you experience the warm hospitality of this quaint community. You will leave revived and refreshed by the wholesome country living.

Rates: $$$ Includes continental plus breakfast. Children are welcome. No pets or smoking, please. We accept MasterCard, Visa, and Discover.

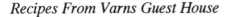

Recipes From Varns Guest House

BREAKFAST COOKIES

1 cup brown sugar	1 teaspoon vanilla
1 cup margarine	1 cup oatmeal
1 cup sugar	1 cup coconut
1 cup oil	1 cup Rice Krispies
1 egg	cereal
1 teaspoon salt	1 cup chopped nuts
1 teaspoon baking soda	3 1/2 cups flour

Mix all ingredients together in large mixing bowl. Shape into round balls and flatten to about 2" across and 1/3" thick. Place on cookie sheet and bake at 350° for 15 minutes. Makes about 3 dozen.

SAUSAGE BRAN CORNCAKE

1 1/4 cups flour	Milk, as needed
3 teaspoons baking powder	1/4 cup vegetable oil
1 teaspoon salt	2 eggs
2 tablespoons sugar	1 cup All-Bran
1 can (8 3/4 ounces) whole kernel corn, drained, reserve liquid	cereal
	24 Eckrich smoky links (2 - 12 ounce pkgs.)

Stir together dry ingredients; set aside. Drain corn; reserve liquid. To reserved corn liquid add enough milk to measure 1 cup. Pour milk mixture, vegetable oil, corn, eggs, and cereal into large mixing bowl. Mix well and add dry ingredients. Pour batter into greased 15 1/2" x 10 1/2" x 1" baking pan, spreading evenly. Arrange smoky links over batter in 2 rows. Bake at 400° for 25 minutes or until lightly browned. Serve warm with maple syrup or cheese sauce. Makes 10 - 12 servings.

The Victoria Bed & Breakfast

206 South Bluff Street • Monticello, IN 47960
219-583-3440
Innkeepers: Steve and Karen McClintock

This 1900 Victorian Queen Anne was built by Karen's great-grandfather, Henry D. Shenk. Five generations of the Shenk family have lived in this home. Located in Monticello's South Historic district, the home is furnished with family antiques, together with treasures Karen and Steve have acquired through the years. Karen's whimsical cow collection is an added attraction not to be overlooked. Three guest rooms with a shared bath are light and airy with ceiling fans, fine linens, and quilts on double beds. Enjoy tempting breakfasts served in the dining room, breakfast room, or on the deck (weather permitting) in view of the grand, old magnolia and maple tree and perennials planted by Karen's grandparents. Close to Lakes Freeman and Shafer, antique shops, and Purdue University.

Rates: $$ Includes continental plus breakfast. Children over age 12 are welcome. No pets, please. Restricted smoking.

Recipes From The Victoria Bed & Breakfast

APRICOT CLAFOUTI

1 cup light cream	1/2 cup all-purpose
2 eggs	flour
6 tablespoons granulated	1 pound fresh apricots,
sugar	pitted & sliced
3 tablespoons chopped	Confectioner's sugar
fresh lemon verbena	

Preheat oven to 350°. Combine cream, eggs, granulated sugar, and lemon verbena with wire whisk until smooth. Gradually whisk in flour. Stir in apricots and pour mixture into lightly buttered 3 cup shallow baking dish. Bake for 30 to 35 minutes or until Clafouti is golden and puffed. Let stand 5 minutes. Dust with confectioner's sugar and serve warm. Makes 4 servings.

MAPLE-CRANBERRY/BLUEBERRY MUFFINS

1 cup all-purpose flour	1 teaspoon baking soda
1 cup unprocessed whole	2 eggs, beaten
bran flakes	1 1/4 cups pure maple
1 cup unsweetened wheat	syrup
germ	1 cup buttermilk
1 teaspoon baking	2 cups cranberries or
powder	blueberries

Preheat oven to 400°. Combine dry ingredients in medium mixing bowl. Set aside. In large mixing bowl, beat together liquid ingredients. Add dry mixture, stirring until just incorporated. Fold in berries. Fill 2" muffin tins 3/4 full with batter. Bake for 15 minutes or until cake tester inserted in center comes out clean. Makes 18 muffins.

Victorian Garden Bed & Breakfast

243 North Walnut Street • Osgood, IN 47037
812-689-4469
Innkeepers: Paul and Linda Krinop

The Victorian Garden is a beautiful 1895 Victorian home located in Osgood. It features golden oak woodwork, gingerbread, pocket doors, and a parlor fireplace. The three bedrooms are all comfortably furnished, clean, cheerful, and air-conditioned. Guests are encouraged to feel at home on the wraparound porch and enjoy the garden gazebo, or sit and bird watch on our patio. Awaken to a coffee tray outside your door. An abundant breakfast featuring freshly baked muffins, seasonal fruits, and special entrees is served in the dining room. Osgood is located in the Southeast corner of the state within 30 minutes of Ohio and Kentucky. We are within minutes of the Versailles State Park, Historic Madison, Friendship - home of the National Muzzle-Loading Rifle Association, and 35 minutes from river boat gambling. Also, visit the many antique shops in our area; many are within walking distance.

Rates: $ - $$$ Includes full breakfast. Children are welcome. No pets, please. Restricted smoking. We accept MasterCard and Visa.

Recipes From Victorian Garden Bed & Breakfast

BREAKFAST CREPE CUPS

<u>Crepes</u>:
1 1/2 cups milk
1 1/4 cups all-purpose
flour
2 tablespoons sugar
3 eggs
2 tablespoons butter,
melted
Dash of salt
1/2 teaspoon lemon
extract (opt.)

<u>Filling</u>:
9 eggs
1/4 cup milk
1/2 teaspoon salt
1/4 teaspoon pepper
6 slices bacon, cooked
crisply & crumbled
1 cup shredded Cheddar
cheese
Sour cream & chives for
garnish

For Crepes: In bowl combine milk, flour, sugar, eggs, melted butter, and salt. Add lemon extract (if desired), beat with mixer until well mixed. Heat lightly greased skillet. Spoon 2 tablespoons of batter into skillet. Brown one side only. Makes 22 crepes. Spray 12 - 2 1/2" muffin cups with Pam. Fit crepes into cups, carefully ruffling the edges. For Filling: Beat together eggs, milk, salt, and pepper. Spoon bacon in the bottom of crepe cups. Ladle egg mixture evenly over bacon. Sprinkle with cheese. Tent foil over muffin cups to prevent overbrowning. Bake at 375° for 25 to 30 minutes or until eggs are set. Carefully remove crepe cups with spoon. Top with a dollop of sour cream and chives. *Freeze remaining crepes between waxed paper, or use as a dessert with fruit. Makes 12 cups.

CHEESE CAKE WITH SOUR CREAM TOPPING

4 - 8 ounce pkgs. cream
cheese, softened
4 eggs
<u>Sour Cream Topping</u>:
1 cup sour cream
2 tablespoons sugar

1 cup sugar
1 teaspoon vanilla

1/2 teaspoon
vanilla

Line bottom and sides of springform pan with favorite graham cracker crust. Cream together cream cheese, eggs, 1 cup sugar, and 1 teaspoon vanilla. Pour into graham cracker crust and bake at 375° for 35 minutes. Remove from oven. Cool for 5 minutes. Mix together Topping ingredients. Pour over cheese cake. Return to oven and bake at 475° for 10 minutes. Remove and cool. Makes 8 servings.

The Victorian Guest House

302 East Market Street • Nappanee, IN 46550
219-773-4383
Innkeepers: Bruce and Vickie Hunsberger

In the heart of Amish country stands this gabled and turreted 1887 Historical Mansion. Etched-glass entry way leads to beveled glass pocket doors and an expansive living room. Elegant Victorian lamps are present here and throughout the home. A wide doorway opens to the dining room with rich wood paneling. The massive 11' dining room table, with a hidden servants' buzzer, is an original piece. Stained glass windows line the dining room and the golden oak staircase. Guests choose from six guest rooms, including the Coppes Suite, with original golden oak woodwork, antique tub, and stained glass. Guests are treated to evening refreshments in their room. Breakfast is an elegant affair, served on china and crystal with cloth napkins. Count on treats like quiche, homemade muffins, fruit, juices, and more. Amish Acres and Borkholder Dutch village are located just one mile from the Inn. "Prepare for a Memory!"

Rates: $$ - $$$ Includes full breakfast. Children are welcome. Limited availability for pets. No smoking, please. We accept MasterCard, Visa, and Discover.

Recipes From The Victorian Guest House

BLUEBERRY FLUFF DESSERT

3 - 3 ounce boxes
raspberry Jello
2 cups boiling water
1 can blueberries, drained

1 cup blueberry juice
1 pint whipping cream
8 ounces cream cheese,
softened

Drain blueberries, reserving 1 cup juice. Dissolve Jello in boiling water. Add blueberry juice. Pour half the Jello into serving dish and refrigerate until firm. Whip whipping cream. Beat in softened cream cheese and remaining Jello to whipped cream. Fold in drained blueberries. Gently pour over first half of refrigerated Jello. Chill until ready to serve.

CHICKEN ROLL-UPS

2 - 8 count tubes crescent
rolls
8 ounces cream cheese,
softened
1/4 cup margarine,
softened
1/4 cup milk
2 stalks chopped celery

2 tablespoons chopped
onion
4 - 5 chicken breast
fillets, cooked &
chopped
10 ounce can cream of
chicken soup
1/2 soup can milk

Separate crescent roll dough into 8 rectangles. Beat cream cheese, margarine, and 1/4 cup milk in mixing bowl until light and fluffy. Stir in celery, onion, and chicken. Spread cream cheese mixture on each rectangle; roll to enclose filling. Place on nonstick baking sheet. Bake at 350° for 18 to 20 minutes or until brown. Mix together soup and half soup can of milk, & warm. Spoon soup over baked roll-ups.

Waterford Bed & Breakfast

3004 South Main Street • Goshen, IN 46526
219-533-6044
Innkeepers: Judith Forbes and Nancy Denlinger

Waterford Bed & Breakfast is located in the heart of Amish country on SR 15 at the south edge of Goshen. Our northern Indiana home is surrounded by two acres which are landscaped with a pleasing variety of trees and gardens. All rooms, which are tastefully and completely furnished with antiques gathered from the Indiana area, include private baths and a full breakfast served with fresh breads and fruits. Nearby attractions include the Wakarusa Maple Syrup Festival, the Amish Acres Art Festival in Nappanee, the Shipshewana Flea Market, the Elkhart County 4-H Fair, the Mennonite Relief Sale in Goshen, and the Notre Dame University located in South Bend. Two rooms are available for guests. Check in time is 4:00 P.M. and check out time is 10:00 A.M., but special arrangements can be made.

Rates: $$ Includes full breakfast. Children over age 8 are welcome. No pets, please. Restricted smoking.

Recipes From Waterford Bed & Breakfast

CORN FRITTERS

2 cups creamed corn
(fresh corn is best)
2 eggs, beaten
2 tablespoons flour

2 tablespoons cream or
milk
Salt & pepper, to taste
4 tablespoons fat

Add beaten eggs, flour, cream, salt, and pepper to the grated corn. Mix thoroughly. Melt fat in frying pan and drop corn mixture by spoonfuls into hot fat. Brown on both sides. Serve with maple syrup. Makes 16 - 18 fritters.

FANCY EGG SCRAMBLE

1 cup diced ham or
Canadian bacon
1/4 cup chopped green
onion
3 tablespoons oleo
12 eggs, beaten
1/2 cup sliced mushrooms

2 tablespoons oleo
2 tablespoons flour
1/2 teaspoon salt
1/4 teaspoon pepper
2 cups milk
4 ounces shredded
Cheddar cheese

Topping:
2 1/4 cups soft bread
crumbs
1/4 teaspoon paprika

4 tablespoons melted
butter

Sauté ham and green onion in 3 tablespoons oleo until tender. Add eggs and scramble until soft-set. Add mushrooms. In separate saucepan melt 2 tablespoons oleo; add flour, salt, and pepper. Add milk, and Cheddar cheese, and cook until bubbly. Gently add cheese mixture to scrambled egg mixture and pour into 12" x 7" greased baking dish. Mix Topping ingredients together and sprinkle on top of egg mixture. Chill. This can be made the night before. Remove from refrigerator 30 minutes before baking. Bake at 350° for 30 minutes. Makes 8 - 10 servings.

Weaver's Country Oaks

0310 North U.S. 20 • LaGrange, IN 46761
219-768-7191
Innkeepers: Rocky and Cathy Weaver

When looking for that bed & breakfast with plenty of elbow room, privacy, good food, and that just-like-home comfort, you are sure to enjoy a stay at **Weaver's Country Oaks**. Located just 5 minutes from Shipshewana, home of one of the country's largest flea markets and auctions. Other activities in the area include biking and touring the many byways of this Amish countryside; or maybe golfing or shopping would be your choice. This two-story home utilizes the second floor for guests with 3 bedrooms, each with it's own bath, a separate kitchen, common room, and breakfast room which opens out to a large stone patio. There is another bedroom with private bath on the first floor. Antique furnishings and quilts are used throughout. Breakfast is served family style with tasty menus of country cooking.

Rates: $$ Includes full breakfast. No pets, please. Restricted smoking. We accept MasterCard and Visa.

Recipes From Weaver's Country Oaks

POTATO PATTIES

2 cups mashed real
 potatoes
2 cups chopped ham
1 cup shredded cheese
1/3 cup margarine
1/4 cup minced onion

1 egg
1 teaspoon prepared
 mustard
1/8 teaspoon ground
 black pepper
Corn Flake cereal crumbs

Put hot mashed potatoes in large bowl. Stir in remainder of ingredients, except Corn Flakes. Chill thoroughly. Form into serving-size patties. Dredge in Corn Flake crumbs. Bake at 350° for 30 minutes. Makes 8 - 10 patties.

WAGON WHEEL SKILLET

4 cups frozen hash brown
 potatoes, thawed
1/4 cup chopped green
 onions
1/2 teaspoon salt
1/4 teaspoon pepper
8 ounces cream cheese,
 softened

2 tablespoons milk
1 pound link sausages
3/4 cup Bisquick mix
1/2 cup milk
1/4 teaspoon ground
 nutmeg
2 eggs
Paprika, to taste

Heat oven to 400°. Grease 10" ovenproof skillet generously. Combine thawed potatoes, onions, salt, pepper, cream cheese, and 2 tablespoons milk in bowl; spread into prepared skillet. Arrange sausages in spoke-like fashion on top. Beat Bisquick, 1/2 cup milk, nutmeg, and eggs with wire whisk or hand beater until almost smooth; pour between sausages. Sprinkle with paprika to taste. Bake until golden brown around the edges, for 25 to 30 minutes. Makes 6 - 8 servings.

Yoder's Zimmer mit Frühstück Haus

P.O. Box 1396, 504 South Main • Middlebury, IN 46540
219-825-2378
Innkeepers: Wilbur and Evelyn Yoder

We enjoy sharing our Amish-Mennonite heritage in our Crystal Valley home. We are within walking distance of downtown, but secluded enough to give our guests privacy. All rooms feature handmade quilts. Antiques and collectibles can be seen throughout the home. Three of our five rooms can accommodate small families. There are several common rooms available for relaxing, reading, TV, games, or socializing. We have an outdoor swimming pool, playground for children, and are air-conditioned. We serve a full homemade breakfast.

Rates: $ - $$ Includes full breakfast. Children are welcome. No pets or smoking, please. We accept MasterCard, Visa, and Discover.

 *Recipes From Yoder's Zimmer mit Frühstück Haus*

MEATBALLS

Meatballs:
1 1/2 pounds hamburger
3/4 cup oatmeal
1 cup evaporated milk
  (Milnot)
3 tablespoons chopped
  onion
1 1/2 teaspoons salt
1/4 teaspoon pepper

Sauce:
1 tablespoon Worcester-
  shire sauce
3 tablespoons vinegar
1 cup sugar
1 cup catsup
1/4 cup water
6 tablespoons chopped
  onion

Mix meatball ingredients together and form into balls. Roll in flour and brown in skillet. Sauce can be heating while you brown the meatballs. Mix all sauce ingredients together and heat through. Pour sauce over meatballs and simmer, or bake at 325° for two hours.

VEGETABLE DIP

1 cup mayonnaise
2 teaspoons minced onion
4 teaspoons soy sauce

1 teaspoon vinegar
2 teaspoons water
Scant teaspoon ginger

Mix all ingredients together a day before serving. Makes a delicious dip for assorted vegetables.

118

Yount's Mill Inn

3729 Old State Road 32 West • Crawfordsville, IN 47933
765-362-5864
Innkeepers: Jerone and Keith Collier

Yount's Mill Inn is located on a beautiful wooded ten-acre site on Sugar Creek, where the Yount Woolen Mill Company operated from 1843 until 1910. **The Inn** building, listed on the National Register of Historic Places, was built in 1851 by the Yount family, as their home and as a boarding house. Walking trails on **the Inn** property provide the opportunity for leisurely strolls along scenic Sugar Creek and Spring Creek. Bicycle country roads, visit local antique shops or see the many historic places in Crawfordsville such as: Wabash College, the General Lew Wallace study where Ben Hur was written, the Old Jail Museum, and the Lane Place, an 1846 mansion on the Historic Register. Our **Inn** has four guest rooms.

Rates: $$ - $$$ Includes full or continental plus breakfast. Children over age 10 are welcome. No pets or smoking, please. We accept MasterCard and Visa.

Recipes From Yount's Mill Inn

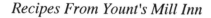

CINNAMON BREAD

1 1/2 cups brown sugar	1 teaspoon salt
2 1/2 cups sifted flour	1/2 cup shortening
2 1/2 teaspoons baking powder	1 teaspoon cinnamon
	1 egg
	3/4 cup milk

Mix together first five ingredients. Reserve 3/4 cup for crumbs and add cinnamon to it. To remaining dough mixture add egg and milk. Spread into square cake pan . Sprinkle crumbs on top of cake & press down into cake with fingers. Bake at 350°; check after 30 minutes.

SAVORY HAM CHEESECAKE

3/4 cup toasted fine bread crumbs	1 cup shredded Swiss cheese
3 tablespoons melted butter, unsalted	1/2 pound chopped ham
3 - 8 ounce pkgs. cream cheese, softened	10 ounces frozen chopped spinach, thawed & squeezed dry
1/4 cup whipping cream	3 tablespoons minced green onions
1/2 teaspoon salt	3 tablespoons melted butter, unsalted
1/4 teaspoon ground nutmeg	1/2 pound mushrooms, cleaned, finely chopped
1/4 teaspoon ground red pepper	Salt & pepper, to taste
4 eggs	

Preheat oven to 350°. Combine bread crumbs and 3 tablespoons melted butter in small bowl. Butter 10" springform pan; press crumbs on bottom of pan. Bake 8 to 10 minutes. Cool. Reduce temperature to 325°. Beat cream cheese, cream, salt, nutmeg, and red pepper until smooth. Beat in eggs one at a time. Split mixture between two bowls. Put half of cheese in each bowl. Add ham to one bowl; add spinach and green onions to the other. Pour spinach filling over cooled crust. Melt 3 tablespoons butter in skillet. Sauté mushrooms over medium-high heat until all moisture evaporates, stirring frequently. Season with salt and pepper. Spoon mushrooms over spinach layer. Pour ham layer over mushrooms. Set pan on baking sheet and bake for one hour. Turn oven off, cool cheesecake in oven for one hour with door ajar. Serve warm. Makes 10 - 12 servings.

Recipes From Yount's Mill Inn

HUNGARIAN COFFEE CAKE

2 sticks butter or
  margarine
2 cups sugar
4 eggs, slightly beaten
2 teaspoons baking soda

2 cups sour cream
2 cups sifted flour
2 teaspoons baking
  powder
2 teaspoons vanilla

Topping:
1/4 cup sugar
2 teaspoons cinnamon

1 cup chopped
  pecans

Cream butter and sugar; add slightly beaten eggs. Add baking soda and sour cream. Gradually add flour and baking powder. Add vanilla. Pour half of batter into greased bundt pan. Sprinkle with half of topping, and cut into batter with a knife. Pour remaining batter into pan and sprinkle with rest of topping, cut this into batter with a knife also. Bake at 350° for one hour. Cool for one hour before removing from pan. Makes 8 servings.

BACON & CHEESE PUFF

8 slices bacon, cooked
2 medium onions,
  chopped
12 slices white bread,
  quartered
1/2 pound Swiss cheese,
  shredded

8 eggs
4 cups milk
1 1/2 teaspoons salt
1/4 teaspoon pepper
Red pepper sauce or
  mustard to taste

Cook bacon until crisp; remove from pan, drain, and crumble. In bacon drippings, cook onions until soft. Arrange half of bread slices in single layer in bottom of greased 9" x 13" baking dish. Sprinkle with half the crumbled bacon, onions, and cheese. Repeat layer with remaining bread, bacon, onions, and cheese. Combine remaining ingredients and pour over layers in pan. Can be prepared in advance and refrigerated until ready to bake. Bake at 375° until set, and top is puffed and golden, about 50 minutes. Makes 8 servings.

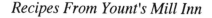

Recipes From Yount's Mill Inn

HONEY BUNS

5 - 6+ cups flour, divided
1/2 cup sugar
1 1/4 teaspoons salt
2 pkgs. dry yeast
3/4 cup milk
1/2 cup water
Topping:
3/4 cup margarine
2 cups packed brown
  sugar

1/2 cup margarine
3 eggs, room temperature
6 tablespoons softened
  margarine & brown
  sugar for filling

1 1/2 cups pecans
3/4 cup honey

Mix 2 cups flour, sugar, salt, and undissolved yeast. Heat milk, water and margarine in pan until warm. Add to dry ingredients. Mix with mixer at medium speed for 2 minutes. Add eggs and 1/2 cup flour, beat for 2 minutes. Stir in enough flour to make a soft dough (do not use over 5 - 6 cups flour). Knead until smooth, about 8 minutes. Place in greased bowl; turn to grease other side. Cover, let rise until double, about 45 minutes. For Topping: Melt margarine and add remaining ingredients; heat until blended. Divide mixture evenly among 3 - 9" cake pans. Punch down dough. Divide into 3 pieces. Roll each out to 9" x 5". Spread with softened butter and brown sugar. Roll up and pinch seams; cut into 2" slices. Cover and let rise. Bake in prepared cake pans at 400° for 20 to 25 minutes. Invert rolls onto serving plate after cooling slightly.

BACON & EGGS AU GRATIN

2 tablespoons butter or
  margarine, melted
1 small onion, finely
  chopped
2 tablespoons flour
1 1/2 cups milk
1 cup shredded Cheddar
  cheese

6 hard-cooked eggs,
  sliced or chopped
10 - 12 slices bacon,
  fried crisply &
  crumbled
1 cup crushed potato
  chips

Sauté chopped onion in melted butter in medium saucepan. Blend in flour; remove from heat, and gradually add milk to blend. Return to heat, stirring constantly until smooth and thickened. Add cheese, stir to melt, and remove from heat. Place layer of eggs in bottom of 1 1/2 quart baking dish. Cover with half of crumbled bacon, then with half of cheese sauce. Repeat layers. Top with crushed potato chips. Bake uncovered at 350° for 15 to 20 minutes or until heated through. Makes 4 generous servings.

Zimmer Haus Bed & Breakfast

130 Orpha Drive • Middlebury, IN 46540
219-825-7288
Innkeepers: Robert and Carolyn Emmert

Visit northern Indiana with cordial, small towns and beautifully kept farms. Experience the many excellent restaurants, gift, craft, and antique shops. Then come home to **Zimmer Haus**, your home away from home - the perfect blend of contemporary styled living with our beautiful country setting. Relax on a porch swing, stroll among the fragrances from our flower garden, or watch our llamas graze and play in the pasture. Retreat to air-conditioned facilities offering two bedrooms with shared bath, a common area with cable TV and a fireplace, all privately set apart from our own living quarters. Top the evening off with complimentary beverages and snacks, and a full breakfast to begin the new day's adventure. Come see for yourself why guests return year after year. Couples, please ask about our "exclusive guest" option.

Rates: $ - $$ Includes full breakfast. Children are welcome. No pets, please. Restricted smoking.

BLUEBERRY BUCKLE

3/4 cup sugar
1/4 cup shortening
1 egg
3/4 cup milk
  (or more)

2 cups sifted flour
2 teaspoons baking
  powder
1/2 teaspoon salt
2 cups frozen blueberries

Crumb topping:
1/2 cup sugar
1/3 cup sifted flour

1/2 teaspoon cinnamon
1/4 cup soft butter

Mix sugar, shortening, and egg. Stir in milk, flour, baking powder, and salt. Blend in blueberries that have been coated lightly in flour. Spread in 9" x 12" glass dish. Batter will be thick. Mix crumb topping ingredients together; sprinkle over batter. Bake at 375° for 45 to 50 minutes, until toothpick comes out clean. Makes 8 - 10 servings.

HASH BROWN QUICHE

3 cups frozen loose-pack
  shredded hash browns,
  thawed
1/3 cup butter or
  margarine, melted
1 cup bacon, browned
  & chopped into small
  pieces

1 cup shredded Cheddar
  cheese
1/4 cup diced green
  pepper (opt.)
2 eggs
1/2 cup milk
1/2 teaspoon salt
1/4 teaspoon pepper

Press hash browns between paper towels to remove excess moisture. Press into bottom and up sides of ungreased 9" pie plate. Drizzle with butter. Bake at 425° for 25 minutes. Combine cooked bacon, cheese, and green pepper; spoon over crust. In small bowl, beat eggs, milk, salt, and pepper. Pour over all. Reduce heat to 350°, bake for 25 to 30 minutes or until knife inserted near center comes out clean. Allow to stand for 10 minutes before cutting. Makes 6 servings.

NOTES

NOTES

ORDER FORM

Indicate the quantity of the book(s) that you wish to order below.
Please feel free to copy this form for your order. For information
please call (812) 663-4948. MAIL THIS ORDER TO:

Winters Publishing
P.O. Box 501
Greensburg, IN   47240

Quantity

_____	Heart Healthy Hospitality	$10.95 each	_____
_____	Mountain Mornings	10.95 each	_____
_____	American Mornings	12.95 each	_____
_____	What's Cooking Inn Arizona	12.95 each	_____
_____	Pure Gold - Colorado Treasures	9.95 each	_____
_____	Colorado Columbine Delicacies	10.95 each	_____
_____	Inn-describably Delicious	9.95 each	_____
_____	Indiana B&B Assn. Cookbook	9.95 each	_____
_____	Hoosier Hospitality	10.95 each	_____
_____	Savor the Inns of Kansas	9.95 each	_____
_____	Sunrise in Kentucky	9.95 each	_____
_____	Another Sunrise in Kentucky	9.95 each	_____
_____	Just Inn Time for Breakfast	10.95 each	_____
_____	Be Our Guest	9.95 each	_____
_____	Palmetto Hospitality - Inn Style	10.00 each	_____
_____	A Taste of Tennessee	9.95 each	_____
_____	Good Morning West Virginia	12.95 each	_____
	Shipping Charge	2.00 each	_____
	5% Sales Tax (IN residents ONLY)		_____
		TOTAL	_____

Send to:

Name: _____

Address: _____

City: _____ State: _____ Zip: _____

Bed & Breakfast Cookbooks
from Individual Inns

*Heart Healthy Hospitality - Low Fat Breakfast Recipes From The Manor At Taylor's
Store Bed and Breakfast Country Inn*
Features over 130 wonderful low-fat breakfast recipes from The Manor at Taylor's Store
in Virginia. Features special lay-flat binding. 160 pgs. $10.95

Mountain Mornings - Breakfasts and other recipes from The Inn at 410 B&B
Features a variety of about 90 tempting recipes from The Inn at 410 B&B in Arizona.
Features special lay-flat binding. 128 pgs. $10.95

More Bed & Breakfast Cookbooks

American Mornings - Favorite Breakfast Recipes From Bed & Breakfast Inns
Features breakfast recipes from 302 inns throughout the country, with complete information about each inn. 320 pgs. $12.95

State Association Cookbooks

What's Cooking Inn Arizona - A Recipe Guidebook of the AZ Assn. of B&B Inns
Features 126 recipes from 21 inns throughout the state of Arizona, with complete information about each inn. 96 pgs. $12.95

Pure Gold - Colorado Treasures / Recipes From B&B Innkeepers of Colorado
Features more than 100 recipes from 54 inns throughout the state of Colorado, with complete information about each inn. 96 pgs. $9.95

Colorado Columbine Delicacies - Recipes From B&B Innkeepers of Colorado
Features 115 recipes from 43 inns throughout the state of Colorado, with complete information about each inn. Features special lay-flat binding. 112 pgs. $10.95

Inn-describably Delicious - Recipes From The Illinois B&B Assn. Innkeepers
Features recipes from 82 inns throughout the state of Illinois, with complete information about each inn. 112 pgs. $9.95

The Indiana Bed & Breakfast Association Cookbook and Directory
Features recipes from 75 inns throughout the state of Indiana, with complete information about each inn. 96 pgs. $9.95

Hoosier Hospitality - Favorite Recipes from Indiana's Finest B & B Inns
Features over 125 recipes from 54 inns throughout the state of Indiana, with complete information about each inn. 128 pgs. $10.95

Savor the Inns of Kansas - Recipes From Kansas Bed & Breakfasts
Features recipes from 51 inns throughout the state of Kansas, with complete information about each inn. 112 pgs. $9.95

Sunrise in Kentucky
Features 100 recipes from 51 inns throughout the state of Kentucky, with complete information about each inn. 112 pgs. $9.95

Another Sunrise in Kentucky
Features 110 recipes from 47 inns throughout the state of Kentucky, with complete information about each inn. 112 pgs. $9.95

Just Inn Time for Breakfast (Michigan Lake To Lake B & B Association)
Features recipes from 93 inns throughout the state of Michigan, with complete information about each inn. Features special lay-flat binding. 128 pgs. $10.95

Be Our Guest - Cooking with Missouri's Innkeepers
Features recipes from 43 inns throughout the state of Missouri, with complete information about each inn. 96 pgs. $9.95

Palmetto Hospitality - Inn Style (South Carolina)
Features over 90 recipes from 47 inns throughout the state of South Carolina, with complete information about each inn. 112 pgs. $10.00

A Taste of Tennessee - Recipes From Tennessee Bed & Breakfast Inns
Features 80 recipes from 40 inns throughout the state of Tennessee, with complete information about each inn. 96 pgs. $9.95

Good Morning West Virginia! - Travel Guide & Recipe Collection
Features 119 recipes from inns throughout the state of West Virginia, with complete information about each inn, and travel information about the state. 160 pgs. $12.95

128

INDEX OF BED & BREAKFASTS

AUBURN
Hill Top Country Inn.................44
BETHLEHEM
Inn at Bethlehem.......................52
BEVERLY SHORES
Dunes Shore Inn B&B...............32
BLOOMINGTON
Bauer House Bed & Breakfast.......16
BROOKVILLE
Sulina Farm Bed & Breakfast.....100
CHESTERTON
Gray Goose Inn.........................40
CRAWFORDSVILLE
Yount's Mill Inn......................118
FISHERS
The Frederick-Talbott Inn..........38
FORT WAYNE
The Carole Lombard House.........26
FRANKLIN
Oak Haven Bed & Breakfast.........72
GOSHEN
Indian Creek Bed & Breakfast......48
Prairie Manor Bed & Breakfast.....88
Royer's 1836 Log House B&B.....90
Spring View Bed & Breakfast......94
Waterford Bed & Breakfast.........112
GREENFIELD
Ahlbrand's Inn..........................10
INDIANAPOLIS
The Nuthatch Bed & Breakfast.....70
The Old Northside B&B..............76
Stone Soup Inn.........................96
JAMESTOWN
Oakwood Bed & Breakfast...........74
JEFFERSONVILLE
1877 House Country Inn.............. 6
KENDALLVILLE
McCray Mansion Inn B&B.........66
LAGRANGE
Atwater Century Farm B&B........14
M & N Bed & Breakfast.............62
Weaver's Country Oaks............114
LAPEL
Kati-Scarlett Bed & Breakfast.......56
LAPORTE
Arbor Hill Inn.........................12

LAWRENCEBURG
The Folke Family Farm Inn........36
LEESBURG
The Prairie House B&B.............86
MADISON
Schussler House B&B...............92
METAMORA
Thorpe House Country Inn....... 102
MICHIGAN CITY
The Hutchinson Mansion Inn......46
MIDDLEBURY
Bee Hive Bed & Breakfast...........18
The Country Victorian B&B.......30
Empty Nest Bed & Breakfast.......34
The Lookout Country Inn..........60
Varns Guest House................. 104
Yoder's Zimmer mit
Frühstück Haus......................116
Zimmer Haus Bed & Breakfast... 122
MILLERSBURG
The Big House in the Little
Woods Bed & Breakfast..............22
MISHAWAKA
The Beiger Mansion Inn.............20
MONTICELLO
The Victoria Bed & Breakfast 106
NAPPANEE
Market Street Guest House.........64
Olde Buffalo Inn B&B...............78
The Victorian Guest House....... 110
NASHVILLE
Orchard Hill Inn & Cabin...........84
Story Inn...............................98
OSGOOD
Victorian Garden B&B 108
PERU
Cole House Bed & Breakfast.......28
RISING SUN
Mulberry Inn & Gardens B&B.....68
SALEM
Lanning House & 1920's Annex..58
SOUTH BEND
The Book Inn Bed & Breakfast.....24
The Oliver Inn B&B..................80
VALPARAISO
The Inn at Aberdeen.................50